The World Odyssey
of a
BALINESE PRINCE

Idanna Pucci

Illustrations by Anak Agung Madé Djelantik
Foreword by Goenawan Mohamad
Preface by Francesco Clemente

TUTTLE Publishing
Tokyo | Rutland, Vermont | Singapore

I dedicate my watercolors to Astri with whom I will be in love even in the afterlife.

Dr. A.A. Madé Djelantik

To Terence Ward, whose presence beside me transforms even the most strenuous task into a poetic experience.

Idanna Pucci

Table of Contents

The Prince

Bali is one of those places where the local is surprisingly universal, not only because the place is treasured, idealized, and exoticized by many but also because its history is marked by events that people from diverse places and times can effortlessly share: beauty and violence, natural disaster and rare delight, innocence and cruelty, the mystery of birth and daily stupidity. All surface often in intense color and resonance like a big production movie.

This book, however, is not another romanticized account of Bali. It is simply a story of a man's life. It is Idanna Pucci's good fortune that she has as her subject a highly unusual man, a person who gathers the local and the global in his singular personality and does it in an unpretentious way. He is not only a prince from Karangasem but also a person whose life was shaped by many different places and uncommon events. He is not only a man who has gone through a long series of historical accidents but also a medical doctor who is blessed with multifaceted talents.

Dr. A.A. Madé Djelantik, whose name in part comes from a ninth-century Balinese word, has seen a twentieth-century European war and a colonized feudal society transformed into a proud, sometimes chaotic, republic. An amazing list of geographical names punctuates his curriculum vitae: Baghdad, Kabul, Buru Island, Mogadishu....

The temptation of this epic is almost irresistible, partly due to the unassuming way Madé Djelantik recounts his remarkable life and partly to Idanna's narration that gracefully moves in the realm of the anecdotal. The interesting thing about this book is that the words do not occupy center stage. In fact, they blend with the visual side of the narrative—a series of watercolors created by Madé Djelantik himself. As visual records of his "memoirs," their nostalgic tone unmistakably suggests a past chronicled with an agreeable lightness of remembering.

A memoir is by no means a self-rediscovery. It is a self-creation, the result of a construction of a narrative coherence. Singular events are organized and transformed into a "poetic" totality, and a plot is born to determine which memories must be included and which ones enhanced. At the end, what we discover is not a full representation of a "self," yet it is just as forceful in revealing truth. And the narrative is an experience from which we learn about "life."

In the case of Madé Djelantik's life and works, as told by Idanna, the learning begins and ends with the thought that it may be a good idea, even in our violent time, to recreate the possibility of joy.

—GOENAWAN MOHAMAD

From East to West

In the tumultuous twentieth century, those born in the 1920s were fated to meet a special destiny. They found themselves face to face with the contemplative knowledge of the ancient Eastern cultures and yet unable to escape a barrage of Western materialistic propaganda.

The wisest members of that generation transmitted to the next generation what was left of their traditions, and their immediate descendants traveled by bus from Istanbul to Peshawar in the seventies seeking new freedoms. Today, the message of those traditions is somehow lost but its spirit survives in unexpected places all over the planet.

I am moved by the deep care with which Idanna Pucci has preserved the memory of a Balinese prince, born in those years under the shadow of a majestic volcano and who journeyed from East to West.

Idanna has lived a long time in Bali. And the island is the cultural equivalent of those gorgeous birds now in extinction because of their beauty and friendly nature.

In Bali, beauty and friendliness find their expression continuously through all the arts. Communication with another world is constant: with the world of the spirits, with nature, and with all those human beings who have passed on.

In her recounting the story of the prince, Idanna highlights, without romanticizing, the calm strength of a society still capable of tangibly feeling the sense of the "sacred" and living with it daily. The prince of these true stories feels the sense of the sacred. He knows how to recognize within the weft and warp of life's material side the threads made up of coincidences, illuminating moments, and miracles.

We are grateful to Idanna and her prince for having reminded us that it is still possible to hear and witness the secret harmony that exists in the world with simplicity, a sense of humor, and above all with great joy.

New York, December 2017

—FRANCESCO CLEMENTE

THE WORLD ODYSSEY OF A BALINESE PRINCE

The last raja of Karangasem, Gusti Bagus Djelantik (1887–1966), with one of his consorts, Ratu Istri Oka Cakrakusuma, and their eldest daughter, A.A. Ayu Winten Cakrakusuma.

The Island That Was

Invisible forces surround us at all times, wherever we may be on this planet. In some cases, these forces intervene at the last minute, just in time to save a human life. In our scientifically oriented Western societies, we tend to brush off such events as mere "coincidences," a stroke of luck. However, the prince and protagonist of these stories referred to these incidents as "good *karma*."

I first arrived in Bali at a time when the few foreigners living there were either artists or anthropologists or storytellers at heart, like myself. The culture attracted me like a magnet and soon I found myself captivated by the ceiling paintings in Kertha Gosa, the historic court of justice in Klungkung, the former royal capital of Bali. My long exploration into the meaning of the 144 paintings led me to settle in East Bali, under the looming shadow of the great Gunung Agung volcano.

It was during this time, many years ago, that I first met Prince Madé Djelantik around a dinner table in the southern coastal village of Sanur in Bali. It would not be out of place to remember that evening with the words "Once upon a time...."

It was in the early 1980s when I drove an old automobile down to the coast from the far eastern hills of Sidemen where I lived in the region of Karangasem, the former kingdom of the Djelantik dynasty.

As soon as I sat next to Dr. Djelantik, I was captivated by the simple ways of this Balinese gentleman with brilliant dark eyes and a smile open to the world. In his presence I felt as if a gust of fresh mountain breeze was blowing in the tropical humidity of the southern coast. He had recently retired from the World Health Organization and had opened a medical practice in his own house in Renon, not far from Sanur. Unless you knew who he was, you could not have guessed from his simplicity and modesty that the prince was one of the most respected and prominent personalities on the island.

I was certain that the simple idea that he existed would enrich my life, as happens when one comes across a truly inspiring book or an experience that changes you.

Our friendship evolved slowly. I was always a bit intimidated by his wife Astri. She was as protective of her man as the mysterious birthmark, hardly visible, in the middle of his neck. This spot was extremely powerful and played a key role in his life, as I would find out later.

Astri was both his guardian angel and his sentinel. And she always spoke her mind. No nonsense. Like him she was already on her way to venerable age. Her face showed the signs of her many adventures as a mother of five, married to a doctor who had been for the most part posted in isolated and distant places, conjuring up images of "banishment" or "exile." Yet, she had made the best of everything, standing by his side, helping him in his mission of healing.

They had fallen in love in Holland in 1943, during the war, in the hospital where she served as a nurse and he worked as a young doctor in training. Astri was an innocent Dutch girl, pretty, blonde with blue eyes and rosy cheeks. She was a force of nature in disguise. I still wonder how that small foreign woman managed to protect him so diligently from the relentless pressure of layers

Madé Djelantik and Astri Zwart on their wedding day.

of family obligations, relationships, cultural clashes, and extensive religious duties—quite an admirable and rare achievement for a Western woman married into a Balinese royal family! And she always kept her calm and sense of humor. Madé and Astri complemented each other and together formed a formidable couple. The doctor, whether in his wife's company or alone, was always modest, generous with his time, ready to hear an amusing story, and eternally curious about everything.

In those days I would find myself wishing I had a magic wand to unlock the treasure trunk that held the secret of his zest for life: a combination of innocence and courage, wisdom and knowledge, traditional values and an open mind and, above all, a compassionate heart. I would visit him and Astri simply to breathe in their unique atmosphere, and I always came away inspired and convinced that my life had been blessed by good fortune.

In my eyes he was two persons in one: a Balinese prince and a Western physician. As a visual witness of "feudal Bali," our prince held the key to the island's stories of the first encounters with the outside world. He was a repository of myths grounded in the most ancient spiritual beliefs in the history of mankind: Animism and Hinduism. One of these myths recounted in great detail the origins of his family, a romantic story par excellence.

Our physician, on the other hand, was a modern-day scientist rooted in Aristotelian reason. A recognized malaria and tropical disease specialist, he was also a born healer. He walked the fine line between East and West, between the ancient culture in which he was born and a Western medical education stubbornly pursued against all odds. He juggled this duality with quiet ease and wisdom like a magician of life, creating bridges between peoples and cultures.

When the prince was born in 1919, the centuries-old world of Bali was still intact, enveloped by constant ritual, thriving in natural beauty with the certainty that the island was the "navel" of the universe. Few in the outside world had heard the word "Bali" or even knew that it was a tiny speck of spectacular volcanic land floating at sea, one of 17,508 islands forming the largest archipelago on earth, known then as the Dutch East Indies and now as the Republic of Indonesia. If superimposed on the map of Europe, this archipelago would stretch from Ireland all the way to the Caspian Sea.

The island of Bali—about 2,230 square miles—washed by the Indian Ocean and the South China Sea, was the only place outside the Indian subcontinent where a microcosm of Hindu faith, blended with Animism, had been flourishing for centuries within a Muslim-dominated world.

Ten years after my first encounter with the prince and about seventy years after his birth, the island was still inhabited by a pantheon of invisible forces. Continuously renewed by daily rituals and prayers—all turned in the direction of the great sacred volcano Gunung Agung—these forces empowered Bali as a place of magnetic energy.

Then, one day I discovered that a surprising bond united me with the prince, one that reached beyond my imagination. It was late afternoon and a pink glow lit the sky. I was sitting on the verandah of my house in East Bali. The gorgeous landscape extended for miles under the splendid dormant Mount Agung. Strewn around on the sofa lay all the documents of our piece of land, a most amazing array of permits and agreements. I had only recently overcome the mandatory initiation into the legal labyrinth of bureaucracy that faces every foreigner who intends to reside for a long time in Indonesia, a process as risky as the trials of Frodo in *The Lord of the Rings*.

That day I was reflecting on my good *karma* as I tidied up all the documents, including a laboratory analysis of our spring water with its long list of minerals. Now, at last, all was in order, thanks also to our generous friend Madé Nasib, builder of the house. Happy and relieved, I felt my soul expand at the realization of being protected by auspicious forces.

I was thinking about the wonderful mysteries of the island when my eyes suddenly fell on a document that I had never really scrutinized—the *Akte Jual-Beli*, literally the Deed of Sale and Purchase—which described the history of the land.

Before the Dutch colonial conquest of Bali in 1908, the Balinese handled all transactions verbally and publicly within the community and village council. Everyone knew everyone else's possessions, which guaranteed a certain security. The Dutch introduced new methods of control along with bureaucracy, and every piece of land, however small, had to be registered. And each time the land changed hands, it was recorded in the *Akte Jual-Beli*, with the date and names of the previous and the new owner, their signatures, and the compulsory stamps.

On the paper I held before me, just two names appeared. One was Pak Ketut Merta, the elderly farmer I knew well, who owned most of the rice fields around the house. Every day I would spot him tirelessly at work. He had parted with this piece of land because he needed funds for a family cremation long postponed. This particular piece was free from the usual obligations and respect given to ancestral land because he had purchased it.

As I read the name of the previous owner, I lost my breath when I saw spelled out clearly "Dr. A.A. Madé Djelantik. Year 1967. Royal Palace of Karangasem. Married." I rubbed my eyes in disbelief. Could this be the doctor I knew?

I had come across this land a few years earlier, in 1991, walking through the countryside. It lay just outside of the village of Ogang, and at that time only a path and a narrow bridge across the Unda River linked it to the other side of the valley. Things had slightly changed since then. Now, even though the area still had no electricity or telephone, an unpaved road had just been prepared to receive a patina of asphalt. How could the doctor possibly have owned such a small patch of land here in the middle of nowhere? And why hadn't he recognized it when he had come to the house for its ritual opening? Or that night when he stayed as our first guest?

It was evening, but I got into the car all the same and drove the two hour distance to the doctor's house, arriving unannounced,

Astri as a young bride in the palace of Karangasem in 1948. Next to her is her first born, Bulantrisna, about two years old. On the left is her husband, Dr. Djelantik, and standing, her father-in-law, the raja.

something quite normal in Bali. Astri's health had become fragile, and to make matters worse she had broken her hip. Despite the circumstances, there was a soothing sense of calm in the air. The doctor took care of his wife with such devotion that the house was filled with the serenity of their love and also their complicity in the face of pain.

I showed him the document. He stared at it pensively.

"Yes, this must be me," he said, looking at his own name in print. Astri, silent at first, then spoke.

"It may be the land we sold to build this house, when you were posted in Iraq," she said, looking at him.

"Ah, yes, you are right," he nodded, "that land from my father." He turned towards me. "It was after independence, when the government introduced land reform and expropriated most of his holdings for redistribution. He gave pieces of land, scattered here and there in the kingdom, to his ten sons, and some also to his farmers. I never even saw what came to me. There were so few roads, we had no idea where it was...."

He went on to explain what I partly knew already, that once upon a time his ancestors ruled all of East Bali. The last king, his father, Anak Agung Agurah Ketut Karangasem, owned 500 hectares of precious land. A generous ruler, he expected from the farmers only rice and coconuts for his family's religious ceremonies, and just enough to feed the royal household of about two hundred people. He even paid the taxes of his tenant farmers. All his subjects loved and respected him, except for his abusive bailiffs who took advantage of his good heart. These corrupt men were ultimately responsible for his financial demise. By the time he died in 1966, the good king had retreated to his cherished residence at Tirta Gangga, surrounded by the beautiful water-gardens that he had created, which he could no longer afford to maintain. The fountains and pools fell into neglect.

"Land reform was a good thing for him," the doctor confessed, "because the bailiffs lost their jobs."

I looked at the wise doctor. He seemed to be at peace with the long gone past and was actually amused by the story of his land ending up in my care. He took it most naturally in typical Balinese style and did not show any sign of surprise.

I thought of that immense man-carved puzzle of rice fields of every color, size, and shape that still graced the region of Karangasem, seemingly left untouched by the events of history. For the most part, the descendants of the king's farmers were still working those fields. But not all of them, like my friend in Ogang, had the good fortune to own the soil they toiled. Several were still tenant farmers and their current landlords were not as generous as the late king.

"Those lands gave us so much," the doctor said, making a sweeping gesture towards the walls of his charming home. "No wonder I slept so well up there in your house!" he added, smiling.

Driving back to East Bali, I could not help feeling that mysterious forces were at work around me. With my husband Terence, I had survived our epic initiation into the legal system, keeping at bay those adverse spirits whose favorite pastime was to test people's *karma*. And now we had also realized that our house, which seemed to rest on the ground like a kite that had lost its wind, was actually planted solidly on propitious soil.

The surprising news of the land drew me closer to the doctor and our friendship acquired a symbolic meaning. Time passed, a few years filled with joys and sorrows. On December 10, 1997, Astri died and, for the first time in fifty years, the prince found himself without his beloved companion. On her deathbed she made him promise to travel around the world to visit their faraway offspring, friends, and the places he loved.

So he left Bali. He first went to Holland and sailed to the island of Vlieland in the North Sea where he and Astri had spent their honeymoon. He reached it on May 31st, their wedding anniversary. He then spent a few days with his only-son, Widur, near Amsterdam. Vienna followed, where one daughter lived. After taking a pause in Venice, he came to Florence, where finally I had the joy of introducing him to my father and my brother. From Italy he flew to New York and then traveled to Connecticut to visit his other daughter. Then he flew to Seattle and San Francisco.

He returned to Bali reinvigorated, ready for a new phase of life, eager to start writing a sequel to his wonderful memoir, *The Birthmark*, which had been published just in time for Astri to hold a copy in her hand.

In all the years of our friendship, I had never seen the doctor unwell. From the first day we met, he seemed to enjoy perfect health, a serene person at peace with God, humanity, and his own conscience.

But then, one day in August 1999, just after his 80th birthday, he volunteered to be a "test patient" for a team of surgeons. At Sanglah Hospital in Denpasar, which he had founded, a colleague from Holland was scheduled to perform a hernia operation with a new method that was guaranteed to be relapse-proof. Dr. Djelantik felt it was time to deal with a hernia that had been giving him trouble for some time.

Surrounded by surgeons and students, our doctor, under local anesthesia, followed the minutest details of the operation. The operation itself was a success. But then, suddenly, he was struck by an infection. And two weeks later, in a critical state, he was transported to the intensive care unit of the hospital in Surabaya, East Java, where he fell into a deep coma.

Diagnosed with a strain of the encephalitis virus, he was kept alive with intravenous feeding. Thirty-five terrible days passed. But, just when the doctors pronounced him lost to the world, the prince woke up, recognized the faces around him, and started to speak with his daughters and son, all reunited around his bed. Incredulous in the face of such recovery, they asked him what he had experienced during his long sleep. But all he could remember was a void.

"You are truly blessed," a Balinese priest later told him. "You reached *moksa!*"

Had the doctor really touched that ultimate spiritual dimension aspired by all Hindus? He could not say. All he knew was that he had gone far away and had returned.

He was unaware then about the strange events that had occurred during his deep sleep. His daughter Trisna, also a medical doctor and a well-known dancer and teacher, was hosting

The raja of Karangasem with his ten children. Madé, the future Dr. Djelantik, wearing a tie is on the right, second row.

at the time a Festival of Indonesian Performing Arts at her grandfather's royal water-gardens of Tirta Gangga. In attendance were three hundred musicians and performers from all over Indonesia.

"Between the various performances," she told me, "we all sat on the grass in meditation, with only father in mind. One night three holy Bissu shamans from South Sulawesi conducted a ceremony to ward off the bad forces that may have caused father's illness.

"We were walking around the gardens with torches when they started swirling around me, singing and swaying their arms, each one holding up high a *kris* dagger, falling into trance. The oldest among them closed me into his embrace and I have no idea for how long all this lasted, but suddenly the sacred dancers came back from their altered state and the oldest shaman told me that father was going to be fine, but this would take some time."

And so it happened. Some inexplicable force brought Dr. Djelantik back at the last hour.

During his convalescence in Java under Trisna's loving care, the prince slowly won back his health and cheerful spirit. Creative by nature, like most Balinese, he was encouraged by his daughter to pursue his one passion: watercolors. In truth, it was painting, not writing, that had always been his secret passion. In the past, whenever free from his professional duties, he had opted for writing, mainly to please Astri. Ironically, his first published works were all about Balinese painting and aesthetics. He now remembered carrying his easel along on his honeymoon. He could still see himself standing with his brushes and watercolors near the tent that he and his bride had pitched on a secluded beach on an island off the northern coast of Holland. But that was fifty-three years ago and he had not painted since.

He chose watercolor as his favorite artistic medium and began to travel back in time, looking at his long life as a sequence of scenes. An explosion of colors blossomed in his mental horizon, a veritable rainbow of pigments awash with water.

Surprisingly, he was not at all intimidated by the medium's fragility, which allows for no errors, and he decided to paint on a large format—20 x 13 inches—like a seasoned watercolorist. The first painting was about his daughter Trisna when, as an infant, she narrowly escaped being eaten for breakfast by an enormous crocodile.

Nine months passed before Dr. Djelantik would return home to Bali, where he closed his medical practice for good. He was now deaf in his left ear and his feet were so unsteady he could hardly control his balance.

I eagerly went to greet him and he timidly brought out five paintings from behind an old easel that was now prominent in the room next to his violin. One by one, he showed them to me without the slightest hint of taking himself seriously, as if painting was simply a new game he had discovered.

I was instantly impressed by what I saw, as if the prince's inner world had suddenly opened before my eyes. In the past I had often found myself listening fascinated to his stories, but to gaze at key moments of his life through his point of view was a much more immediate experience. I was so taken by the scenes that I urged him to continue painting. "And if you do," I said, "we can make a book of your life stories and illustrations."

A few days later I left Bali. After some months spent between Florence and Iran, where my husband had spent his childhood, finally we returned to the island. We drove straight from the airport to Dr. Djelantik's house. His radiant smile welcomed us as he announced that during our absence he had worked non-stop. Then he unveiled his treasures—forty-three watercolors.

With his blessing, we loaded all the precious works into our vehicle and drove up to Ogang. Once home, on "his land," we arranged the paintings one next to the other along the walls of the house in the covered walkways open to the immense vista. And there it was, the most amazing exhibition we could ever have imagined. The neighboring villagers stopped by and scrutinized the scenes as if they were reading the script from a traditional palm leaf *lontar* book.

This collection of stories was born then and there, as if the invisible hand that had reached out nudging the prince to create these scenes had also appointed me to become his messenger.

Turning these pages, one after the other, is like entering a temple in Bali. First, we must clear our mind and prepare to leave behind all daily concerns. Only then can we climb the stairs and pass through the narrow gateway that leads into the inner sanctum where dwell the invisible forces that guide all lives.

In the same spirit, the narrative of this book invites us to first discover the *Romantic Origins* of the prince's ancestors. How can we follow his life journey unless we know something about the ancient myths of his family?

As an adult, after ten years spent in Holland, when the prince returned to his father's palace and listened to the elders reciting the legends, he could not help but be skeptical. He did not really believe in anything he heard, but he kept this to himself because it was unwise—and unthinkable—to contradict the elders for whom these myths represented an unquestionable truth.

In private, of course, he discussed these matters with Astri, whose Dutch common sense never ceased to surprise him.

"Madé," she would say, "tell me, why should it bother you whether these stories are fantasy or fact? For me, this is not important."

"That's fine," he would reply, "but how can you take for truth Gusti Ayu's 'immaculate conception'...?"

"It doesn't matter," Astri would answer. "Isn't it a fact, for instance, that your ancestors conquered the island of Lombok and ruled over its eastern region for more than three hundred years? The dates and the events may not have happened exactly as we are told, but these legends have some validity. The truth lies in their 'spirit,' she insisted. After all, these stories are filled with poetry and suspense. Let's enjoy them, and why not even try to believe them!" But the doctor continued to be perplexed.

One day, much later, after Astri had passed away and he was about to paint the scene of an ancestral story, he thought back to her words. And then, spontaneously, his family myths came back to him, crystal clear, as if he were back in the palace as a child when these legends were for him like a second skin.

The prince's first memory as an infant child—a story called *A Vision*—is his first life story in the collection. This dramatic moment re-emerges in vivid, luminous pastel colors. In a Western context, this terrible event would have affected a child forever.

But, Dr. Djelantik told me, the contrary had happened. He said that in Bali the "individual" must not be viewed in isolation but is always protected by family, community, culture, and the universe.

"The main difference between East and West," he pointed out, "stands in the way the 'individual' is perceived. On one side is the awareness of the collective 'We'; on the other, the all-important ego-oriented 'I'. In our culture, the 'individual' is self-effacing, finding identity and values only as part of a larger community. The solitude that so often I noticed in big Western cities cannot exist in a place where the arrival and departure of a soul are rejoiced for and grieved by everyone."

His words were so true. I had so often realized that whenever I spoke with someone in nearby Ogang, even though I was confronted with a single person, I felt that I was facing his entire village. And yet we both shared the same human condition, the joys, hopes, and insecurities of youth, and the pains of old age.

"The feeling of 'shame' is also a very Eastern emotion," the doctor pointed out. "It has nothing to do with the feeling of 'guilt'. There is a big difference between the two."

He had lived long enough in the West and now he spoke almost as an anthropologist. I thought again about his courage when he embarked on his great adventure across the vast ocean

Prince Madé Djelantik with his brothers.

that separated two entirely different ways of relating to the outside world.

"Shame," he continued, "leads to public disgrace, not only for the person directly concerned but also for his family and community, which is why 'saving face' is so important in our culture. 'Guilt' is the opposite. It is a very private, very Western emotion that does not involve anyone else but the individual who experiences it."

Where did the prince's calm and joyful spirit come from? Perhaps it all had to do with a crucial event in his childhood, when a wise old man with a long white beard announced that the destiny of the little boy would always be tied to an invisible protective force. That auspicious omen, described in the story *A Prophetic Sign*, drives the entire narrative.

And who was that wise old gentleman who had uttered the prophetic words? He was none other than the great poet Rabindranath Tagore, who once stayed as a guest of his father in the royal palace of Karangasem.

So, with Tagore's blessing, let us now start at the beginning with the doctor's royal family origins. Every now and then, the prince's magic spell will rise from these pages and gently touch your heart. It is actually his invisible armor that has always shielded him from danger. Until the very end, during his youthful old age, our eminent Madé Djelantik seemed to glide through life as if he were crossing a flowery meadow in springtime.

"... every single thing, every place, every event has its own inner psychological meaning beyond the apparent one. Every visible image has its own invisible counterpart that evokes in us a much deeper and truthful reality than the one we experience through our senses. This is why symbols, myths, and legends are so meaningful. They lead us beyond the mere visible."

—TIZIANO TERZAN

ROMANTIC ORIGINS

The history of the royal house of Karangasem is filled with mystery and wonder. The most romantic anecdote dates back to 1678, to the founding of the ancestor temple. In those days the kingdom was ruled equally by three brothers who reigned together in perfect harmony over the land as kings. However, the story is not about them but about their only sister, the beautiful Gusti Ayu Nyoman Rai Inten.

One day the three kings were struck by great sorrow when they learned the shocking news that their beloved sister was pregnant. She had barely come of age and sadly no young man had stepped forward to take responsibility. This was a terrible embarrassment for the kingdom. The brothers were overcome with grief because they knew that, according to traditional law, an unwed pregnant princess was punished with death.

During her public interrogation, Gusti Ayu spoke with great calm and insisted that the father of her child was the god of Mount Agung. The audience listened in rapt attention, amazed by her strange story. The kings could not conceal their surprise when she challenged them to believe her. She ended her defense saying that she was certain that the god of Mount Agung would come to visit her that night because the moon was full. Then they could see with their own eyes that she was telling the truth.

That very night of *purnama*, the full moon, a highly sacred moment in Bali, the three kings, with their soldiers armed with *kris* and spears, stood guard around the cottage of Gusti Ayu in the palace of Kelodan. The air was fresh. A soft breeze blew from the sea while the moon shone like a diamond disk over all children and adults on the island, over every pebble and leaf. The mighty mountain to the north stood majestically, dark against the silvery night sky. Under the bright moonlight no one could possibly approach Gusti Ayu's compound without being seen. The door had been left open. A burning oil lamp inside allowed the guards to catch a glimpse of the princess sleeping in her bed. Hours passed and nothing unusual happened.

But suddenly, in the middle of the night, all heads turned towards the sacred volcano. A ball of fire rose from the mountain top and crossed the great expanse of sky, descending over forests and rice fields in the direction of the royal palace. As it approached, all eyes opened wide in wonder and awe. Finally, it landed on Gusti Ayu's roof, where it lingered like a lantern glowing with sapphire light. Instantly, an intoxicating scent of jasmine filled the air.

Soldiers posted on the front porch of the house heard voices inside. Gusti Ayu was talking with someone who had a distinct male voice! As soon as the guards tried to peer inside the open door, the oil lamp went out. When they backed away, the flame burst on again. Soon everyone in the courtyard realized that they were witnessing a supernatural phenomenon. So they gathered at a respectful distance and quietly listened to the two voices whispering like love birds.

All night long the mysterious ball of fire floated above the house as the jasmine fragrance filled the cool evening hours. When the new day came and the sun rose, the kings apologized profusely to their beloved sister and announced with great joy that she was free.

Gusti Ayu's son was named Anak Agung Alit Sakti, the magic child. And very soon the entire court understood that the little boy was endowed with an extraordinary intellect. When he was eight years old, he told his uncles that he could no longer stay with them.

"The time has come for my mother and I to leave the palace of Kelodan," the prince said, and asked the kings to build a residence for his mother on top of a hill, known simply as *bukit* or hill, three miles away. But that was not all. He insisted that this home should be designed like a temple, not a royal palace. Knowing full well that their nephew was of divine origin, the kings granted his wish.

Construction on the hill started immediately. The workers labored day and night and completed the temple in only one month.

When the auspicious day came to leave the palace, Gusti Ayu and her son set out on foot on the path to their new home. The three kings, in their finest sarongs woven in gold thread, followed with their retinue of court attendants. The journey was all uphill. When the trail became too steep, Gusti Ayu reached down and picked up a branch of a *kepel* tree and used it as a walking stick. Her pace quickened and soon she was walking much faster than everyone else. Alit Sakti, holding his mother's hand, effortlessly put one foot in front of the other. With each step the distance grew from their escorts. Even a black dog that had joined the procession was not able to keep pace with them.

Everyone was surprised at the speed of their ascent. Mother and son seemed as swift as the *kokokan* white herons gliding in the wind. Eventually, only two tiny silhouettes could be seen in the distance, reaching the top of the hill.

Exhausted and out of breath, the royal procession finally arrived at the summit. As they entered the temple, the kings and their followers looked about and could not believe their eyes.

The place was deserted. In vain they searched for their sister and nephew but there was no trace of them. People from nearby villages on the slopes soon joined in the search that continued far and wide all afternoo. Yet, astonishingly, both mother and son had vanished.

Not all was lost. Gusti Ayu's walking stick had been left behind. It stood firmly planted in the ground at the center of the temple. Shortly after, the branch sprouted roots that reached deep into the sacred earth. In time, the stick grew into a majestic tree.

> "O profound, silent tree,
> by restraining valor with patience,
> you revealed the creative power
> in its peaceful form.
> Thus we come to your shade
> to learn the art of peace,
> to listen to the word of silence..."
>
> —TAGORE

Today, after over five hundred years, the tree still towers over the Bukit Temple at the exact same spot where Gusti Ayu and Alit Sakti reached *moksa* and the freedom from the cycle of reincarnation.

Mysterious phenomena were soon attributed to the *kepel* tree. The most impressive took place during the legendary conquest of Lombok, an island east of Bali.

Fourteen years had passed since Gusti Ayu's disappearance when, one day, an unexpected visitor arrived by sea requesting an audience with the three kings. He was the leader of a revolt. Braving the dangerous strait separating Lombok from Bali, he had come to ask help from the royal brothers in overthrowing the cruel king of Seleparang.

People in Karangasem, of course, were well aware of Lombok. On a clear day everyone could spot the top of its volcano Rinjani rising high above the horizon. Many legends were attached to its eruptions, to the wild population inhabiting the east coast, and to the intrepid sea-gypsies who worshipped the god of the crescent moon and roamed the eastern shores. But how could the kings deny a request that carried the promise of lands further east?

Finally, the second king volunteered for the mission. Before departing he went up to the Bukit Temple to take leave of Alit Sakti and ask for his blessing. As he prayed under the huge shadow of the *kepel* tree, the divine spirit of his nephew spoke to him: "You must not mobilize a great army. Once you reach the other side, Alit Sakti will come to your assistance." The brave king bowed as a sign of obedience. He then sailed off from the beach in Ujung with only four royal *prahu*.

As soon as they were out at sea, something incredible happened. Thousands of tiny yellow butterflies appeared out of nowhere to lead the way. Flying ahead, they flapped their wings frantically and guided the small Balinese fleet across the rough waters of the Lombok Strait. Thanks to the swarms of yellow butterflies, the vessels braved the notoriously dangerous waves that all mariners feared.

They landed at dawn on the beach of Batu Bolong on the western coast, and nothing could have prepared the king for what happened next. In less than a split second, the butterflies shed their wings and transformed into soldiers, ready for battle. The enemy king fled before the huge advancing Balinese army, and the conquest of Lombok was an easy affair.

According to legend, these butterflies and brave warriors were none other than the yellow leaves from the sacred *kepel* tree.

Turning these pages, one after the other, is like entering a temple in Bali. First, we must clear our mind and prepare to leave behind all daily concerns. Only then can we climb the stairs and pass through the narrow gateway that leads into the inner sanctum where dwell the invisible forces that guide all lives. And now it is our turn to walk up the steps and enter the temple of Kebon Bukit where these life stories are safely enshrined.

A VISION

P rince Madé Djelantik was born on July 21, 1919 in the royal palace of Karangasem, the town today called Amlapura on the far eastern coast of the island of Bali. His mother, Mekelé Selaga, from the *sudra* farming caste, lived far from the king's private chambers, reception pavilions, ceremonial courtyards, and guest rooms. Each of the ten royal wives had her own private quarters where she resided with her children and servants. Her proximity to the king's compound depended on her caste at birth: the higher the caste, the nearer to the king.

No portrait or photograph exists of Madé's mother. She died when he was three years old and the prince does not remember the shape of her face, the touch of her hand, or the gentle light of her eyes.

His father, the king, had been advised by a Western-educated doctor that it would not be safe for Mekelé Selaga to have another baby because she had suffered so greatly during her last childbirth. The risk of hemorrhage, the doctor said, was far too high. The king loved her and most certainly heeded the doctor's advice, using traditional methods of birth control. Yet soon after the sudden death of the youngest baby, Madé's mother was pregnant again.

Months later, her delivery came sooner than expected. In the darkness of that fateful evening, great tension was in the air. In Bali, superstition always prevails during critical moments when life is at risk. Servants rushed to and from the delivery room carrying pails of water, trays and more trays of offerings, and baskets of cloth. Two traditional midwives (usually male healers) stood at Mekelé Selaga's side. Amidst a flurry of activity, six-year-old Princess Ayu Manik, Madé's sister, found her way into the forbidden room. She snuck inside and from a corner saw her mother squatting on the floor holding onto a heavy rope that hung from the ceiling. Two women supported her from behind while two other healers knelt in front of her. Suddenly, a newborn baby's cry pierced the night and the little girl watched as her mother gasped for air and let go of the rope. But just then, quickly an arm reached down and lifted Ayu Manik out of the room.

Meanwhile, three-year-old Madé slept peacefully in the arms of his nanny who sat in a nearby pavilion. The palace courtyards were crowded with people anxiously waiting in the shadows. As time passed some fell asleep, others chatted quietly.

When the first light of dawn streaked its glowing hues across the eastern sky, young Madé woke up and opened his mouth, like a newly born bird. Then, without warning, he began to shriek, waving both arms upwards. All ears and eyes turned towards him. The nanny tried desperately to calm him. But all her efforts were in vain.

The little boy kept screaming wildly: "*Eee, eke, eee... goak... goaaak... Mek pelaibangé... Mek pelaibangé....* Crows.... Help! Don't take her away!"

Everyone looked up at the dawn sky. They saw nothing. No crows flying. Not a cloud. Nothing. But then they all panicked because the body of the little prince started to twitch from side to side in convulsions. The nanny wiped his hot forehead with a wet cloth. Nothing could alleviate the child's despair. Everyone present believed that the evil spirits of the night had taken possession of him. A priest arrived on the scene and began to sprinkle holy water over the boy and the crowd, reciting special incantations to exorcise the alien forces.

Madé quietened down in a matter of minutes and the onlookers breathed great sighs of relief. But then, hushed voices began spreading tragic news. Sweet Mekelé Selaga had passed away. A wave of shock overwhelmed the crowd when all realized that Madé's terrifying despair had coincided with the instant of his mother's death. A stunned silence gripped the entire palace.

Madé and his sister Ayu Manik were soon taken in and cared for by Mekelé Trena, another royal wife. She had recently lost a baby son in tragic circumstances and little Madé quickly filled her void.

PET MONKEY

A wonderful black monkey once lived in the palace. Mekelé Trena, Madé's adopted mother, loved him like one of her own children. This highly intelligent monkey dragged his very long arms comically behind, and everyone, even the king, enjoyed his friendly company.

Without a care in the world, the monkey swung from tree to tree across the royal courtyards, showing off his trapeze virtuosity. The palace was for him like a circus under the great sky. Over time he acquired a reputation for having "semi-divine" powers.

One day, not long before Madé's foreboding hallucination of crows, Mekelé Trena's newly born baby Rai was sleeping peacefully on the verandah. The monkey came lazily down from a tree, lifted the baby out of the cradle, and lovingly began to rock the child, waddling around the porch in the way the nanny always did.

A girl on her way to the spring saw the monkey holding the little prince and burst out with loud screams that echoed beyond the palace walls. Startled, the monkey leapt onto the nearest frangipani tree as people frantically rushed to the scene. They did not entice him to descend by offering a banana or some other monkey delicacy but yelled out in panic, throwing stones and waving sticks in his direction. Terrified, the monkey climbed even further up the tree. When he reached the highest branch

and could go no further, he did the unthinkable. He let go of the child. The baby dropped like a rag doll in a thirty-foot fall.

Little Rai died instantly. The monkey, however, did not run away. He slowly climbed back down to the verandah where he let himself be captured. The question of his innocence was never even raised by the priests and elders who met in a circle to discuss his fate. By sundown they had reached their verdict. The monkey was sentenced to death. The procedures of his punishment took into account his privileged status in the palace.

The monkey was executed with with a single stroke of a ceremonial *kris* on an astrologically chosen day. He was then buried at exactly the same spot where the child had fallen to his death. A huge stone carried all the way from the holy mountain was placed on his grave.

Mekelé Trena was still grieving the tragic loss of her baby boy and also the sad end of her pet monkey when young Madé lost his mother. So, in some way it was thanks to this monkey that she gladly adopted her stepson, giving a younger brother to her first-born son Gedé, the crown prince.

In time, the monkey's gravestone came to be treated with care and respect. Offerings were laid on it regularly on the fifth day of the Balinese five-day week, and also at *tilem*, when each month the moon lapsed to pitch black and blended with the night sky. It was then that the lower spirits were said to roam the island freely in the dark.

A PROPHETIC SIGN

By 1925 a captivating new sport called soccer had rounded the Cape of Good Hope and crossed the Indian Ocean to reach the traditional Hindu world of Bali. Enthusiasm for the game had spread like wildfire across the island, thanks to the much venerated champion team of the Dayaks in the faraway capital of Badung, now known as Denpasar.

Six-year-old Madé loved soccer and played frenetically inside the palace on the large earthen grounds that lay between the royal mothers' compounds. Kicking back and forth unripe grapefruits or balls made of crumpled paper held by string, he frolicked with the servants' children and his many brothers, dreaming of scoring the winning goal.

One memorable day, Madé and his older half-brother Gedé, the crown prince, received a gift they had long wished for. The king handed them a red rubber ball that he had bought in the northern coastal port of Singaraja. Unable to contain their excitement, the two brothers and their friends immediately started kicking it about and madly chasing after it.

A favorite time to run wild was the afternoon. And once, during the spirited mayhem of a dozen swirling legs, little Madé booted the ball with all his strength towards the goal. The ball soared high above two trees, high over the red brick wall, until it disappeared into his father's quarters.

And where was the king at that precise moment? He was sitting on a mat in the central pavilion, on the verandah, with an impressive visitor with a white beard, who was clad all in white like a Brahmin priest. Surprisingly, the ball bounced above his head before coming to rest behind him. The king did not seem to notice and continued to recite aloud from the *lontar*, the narrow strips of engraved palm leaf that form traditional Balinese books.

The ball vanished from view and all the children stood frozen in place, looking at Madé. The servants also turned to stare at him. The little prince ran to peer through the gate and his big dark eyes opened wide in fear! His cherished ball, how could he ever go and fetch it? He was in trouble! Tossing anything over the head of a Brahmin or even his own father was taboo, against all traditional etiquette. And to make matters worse, the ball was "unclean," having touched feet and ground.

Madé was very embarrassed. All he wanted to do was run away and hide. But he knew that it was up to him and no one else to retrieve the precious ball. He gathered up all his courage and crossed the threshold of his father's compound. When he finally reached the verandah, he hesitantly climbed up the few stairs, bowing respectfully, his eyes downcast. Trembling like a leaf, he stammered out words of apology and humbly asked permission to get the ball. To Madé's relief, the king nodded his consent without even looking up, and continued reading to the eminent listener.

Madé crept across the floor on his knees. He kept his head bowed as low as possible so as not to be above the high ranking gentlemen sitting cross-legged. With his heart pounding, he finally reached the ball and rolled it onto his lap. Then, bringing his hands up, palms joined in a sign of respect, he asked to be excused.

Ever so carefully he moved backwards so that the soles of his feet would be turned away from the king, just as the servants

did. But just then, a great hand suddenly grabbed his arm. He peered into the old man's penetrating eyes.

"Your Highness," the guest spoke, "is this a son of yours?"

"Yes," the king replied, looking at little Madé with his eyebrows raised. "Why do you ask?"

"The boy carries an auspicious mark," the old man said. His elegantly long index pointed straight at the boy's neck. "This," he explained, "is a very important sign."

Madé was now truly terrified. He was not accustomed to so much attention and had no idea what the visitor was saying. Wilting under his father's gaze, he dared not move.

"How do you know this?" the king asked surprised.

The guest with the white beard drew Madé even closer, indicating a dark spot between Madé's collar bones.

"Your son is blessed," he said. "He will meet many dangers in life but he will never be harmed. You must not be afraid for him. He enjoys special protection."

The king stared at his son's birthmark in silence. Madé's heart pounded under his father's scrutiny. Time seemed endless. Deep in thought, the king then shifted his eyes back to his book and turned to a new page, dismissing his son with a gentle smile and a flick of the wrist.

Elated and free, Madé ran back to his playmates, holding up the rubber trophy. Loud and spirited cheers greeted his triumph. And with a strong kick he passed the red ball over to his brother Gedé. The game began anew.

THE LOYALTY TEST

O ver time young Madé became so attached to his elder half-brother that he obeyed his every command. In turn, Crown Prince Gedé came to trust Madé implicitly. Together they sat for hours at night watching shadow plays performed by the court puppeteer. This gentleman, whom everyone called *dalang*, was the supreme messenger from the ancestor world, a Brahmin master medium who bridged past and present. His extraordinary storytelling educated the young and reminded the old about *karma*, the inevitable consequences of daily actions.

Every evening the two boys and their numerous brothers and sisters, along with the children of the servants, would gather in front of his quarters and beg the puppet master for yet another story. The *dalang* never refused and they all loved him for it. He would improvise, sometimes using his own hands against a white cloth screen back-lit by an oil lamp. However, on religious occasions he would always perform a grand shadow play for the whole court, lasting from sundown to sunrise.

The living shadows of the mythic heroes from the *Ramayana* and *Mahabharata* epics mesmerized the two boys. When they drifted off to sleep, the *dalang*'s recitations, mixed with hypnotic percussion sounds, entered their dreams.

Gedé saw himself as Rama, whose personification of *dharma* suited perfectly his kind and tolerant nature, so soft-spoken and patient. Madé instead loved Rama's younger brother, Laksamana, and worshipped him for his truth, loyalty, sense of justice, and vigilant courage. With each passing day, the two brothers did their best to emulate the ideals of their favorite heroes.

The king was, of course, pleased with these two sons: Gedé, gentle and thoughtful; little Madé, always ready to protect his older brother and help with anything. But no one truly understood the intensity of their bond. The brothers were each other's idols.

One day it was suddenly announced that Gedé would continue his studies at the Dutch Indonesian school in faraway Badung, in the southwestern part of the island. Madé felt his whole world was coming to an end. His plea to join Gedé was firmly rejected by his adopted mother. Days of confusion and uncertainty followed. The crisis tormented also the crown prince because he could not imagine life without his beloved brother. He began to wonder if Madé was really like Laksamana. Could he be trusted forever?

As their separation grew nearer by the day, Gedé finally decided to put Madé through the ultimate test of loyalty.

"Will you stand perfectly still," he asked, "if I pee on your head?"

"Of course," Madé answered, without hesitation.

So they agreed on the ritual. It would take place on the large tombstone of the mythical monkey whom everyone sorely missed. It was difficult for six-year-old Madé to climb the slippery stone but he accomplished the task without complaining. Standing perfectly straight, he then turned to face the high porch where his brother waited, ready to begin the initiation.

Madé brought both palms together in the *mustika* gesture of religious meditation, and with his eyes cast downward at the stone he fell into deep concentration. Soon Gedé's urine came splashing down like a warm shower. His heart exalted! The

continuous stream running down his cheeks and over his lips had a sour taste. It poured like rain, leaving him drenched.

When it all stopped, Gedé hugged and praised his brother and promised him the unthinkable; he would personally ask their father if Madé could join him in the same school.

The immediate aftermath of that ceremony, however, proved to be painful for little Madé. His adoptive mother, Mekelé Trena, was so angry with him for coming home smelly and wet that she pinched his thighs with all her might, a far more excruciating punishment than slapping or beating but one considered more appropriate for high-caste children.

In contrast, the king was so impressed by Madé's unwavering loyalty that he honored the crown prince's request and agreed not to separate the two brothers. Their ritual on the monkey's gravestone would soon lead Madé into a great adventure filled with countless implications.

BLESSING MINERVA

Minerva was her name. Magnificent and stately, she was manufactured in Belgium before World War I and served proudly as the king's official automobile. Many residents in the kingdom were mystified by this amazing invention that had arrived so far from the cold lands of Europe. Minerva first came to Madé's father as a symbolic gift from the Dutch government in 1910, four years after their conquest of Bali. Once the kingdom of Karangasem had fallen under colonial control, and the king was appointed *Stedehouder* or representative of Queen Wilhemina of Holland, Minerva braved her way across the Java Straits to East Bali.

Bright yellow, the color of Vishnu, this motorcar had a wonderfully spacious cabin that could seat six guests and protect them from the sun under its solid black roof. In Madé's eyes, however, its real beauty lay in all the sparkling brass that glowed gaily, from the large handbrake next to the driver's seat to the beautiful lanterns, the windscreen frames, the radiator, and even the two horns with red rubber balls on either side.

Climbing into Minerva for the first time, Madé could barely contain his excitement. The door opened and a lush dark green dreamworld greeted him. He stared at the thick velvet seats, satin curtains, and silk ceiling. He marveled at the delicate bottles

of eau-de-cologne and a crystal bowl with floating rose petals. In the front he saw the chauffeur turn and nod at him, while his assistant sat proudly in the other seat. If this chariot had wings it would fly he thought.

He knew that he and Gedé were scheduled to leave the palace the following morning and travel to distant Badung to begin their schooling. Noble Minerva would carry them all the way. For weeks, preparations for the long journey had occupied the wise men of the palace. First, a particularly propitious date had to be chosen to protect the young travelers, who would be exposed and vulnerable to unknown forces. Such a day could not be selected randomly or picked simply to coincide with the first day of the school year, July 1, 1925. A specialist had to be consulted. The court priest studied the traditional calendar, numerous horoscopes, and then announced the perfect day to travel: exactly two weeks before classes. When the princes' escorts heard this, they were pleased because the boys would have plenty of time to adjust to their new life in the bustling capital.

Before the big journey, the royal brothers had to ask the gods for permission to leave as well as protection en route. Young Madé was quite impressed at the spiritual preparation that was needed. Each day he and Gedé offered their special prayers. They paid homage to the gods by visiting seven temples in the kingdom. They spent three days on a pilgrimage, which took them also to a mist-covered mountain peak where Madé saw with his own eyes the sacred grove of golden bamboo that held holy water in its shoots.

This temple, Lampuyang, was by far his favorite, even though the climb was very steep and long. From the summit he scanned the blue waters to the west and east. And he could clearly see the wave-tossed Lombok Straits where his brave ancestor had once sailed in a swarm of yellow butterflies.

Of course, great care was taken in arranging offerings to placate the evil spirits that were believed to lay in wait during the trip. Madé noticed that special gifts were crafted for the gods of Candi Dasa and Goa Lawah, two important holy stops along the way. And finally, on the last evening, a grand ceremony was held in the family temple.

Dawn shed its fresh light the morning of their departure. Madé woke with a start. His heart pounded with excitement. Outside the main gate a large crowd had already formed. On a ceremonial platform the high priest punctuated his incantations with the crisp ringing of his silver bell. The blessing of Minerva had begun. Burning incense sticks curled sweet trails of smoke around the brightly shining vehicle. Colorful offerings and flower garlands covered its yellow hood.

Followed by their entourage, the two boys descended the palace steps leading to the street. They sat down below the officiating priest to the left of brassy Minerva. With their legs crossed in lotus position, they faced towering Mount Agung in prayer. The priest sprinkled holy water like a gentle mist that fell over the king, his two sons and their escorts, and over Minerva's chassis. Then the young princes stepped into the car. And slowly the picturesque caravan began to move.

Like a golden carriage of bygone times, Minerva led the way, draped in a blanket of flowers that hung over the windows. The fragrant *cempaka* and frangipani blossoms filled Madé's senses. Welded onto Minerva's hood, a brass toy airplane sprouted proudly above the flowers. When the car advanced, the small propeller started to turn, catching speed as the driver accelerated. Three vehicles followed behind: a Dodge, a Chevrolet, and a Ford, also decked out with cascades of woven palm leaf ornaments.

Lines of people stood on each side of the road, their eyes mesmerized by the splendid procession, trying to catch a glimpse of their king and his two departing sons. The blessed Minerva was spiriting young Madé away on his maiden voyage beyond the ancient kingdom of his ancestors.

FIGHTING COCK BASKETS

In the capital Badung, among the strange things that the young princes of Karangasem saw, nothing was more bizarre than the white people from Holland. At school, strange rumors circulated. White people, Madé heard, were descended from the giant *raksasa*, those frightening demons in the shadow plays who scared all the children. The Dutch Queen Wilhemina, instead, was believed to be directly related to Wibisana, the good, noble brother of the wicked King Rahwana.

Like all their school friends, the Djelantik brothers were filled with insatiable curiosity about the customs of the light-skinned men and women who wore heavy leather boots and wide-brimmed hats, drank large amounts of alcohol, spoke loudly, and sat in chairs. Only seldom, Madé noticed, did they ever smile. And in the heat of the day, they also played a most exhausting game that no one could understand. It was called tennis.

The boys spent hours debating the colors of white skin, which turned from pink to blister red when burned by the sun, like the fiery hot peppers of Bali. They marveled at the impressive shapes of the men's rounded bellies, so similar to those of Twalen and Merdah, the favorite shadow play characters of all children. Both Madé and his brother felt that an abyss separated these white people from their own. This gap seemed as wide as the great Indian Ocean that these strangers had crossed to reach the island.

But one question kept recurring. What was the secret of Dutch women? Why were their hips so much larger than any other white ladies? It remained a perplexing mystery. According to one rumor, under the long skirt each woman wore a bell-shaped rattan basket like those used by Balinese farmers as cages for their fighting cocks. Days passed, and whenever the subject was raised, all of Madé's friends shared the same view: Dutch ladies wore baskets.

"Fighting cock baskets hidden under the skirts? I just don't believe that!" Madé would tell his mates. But they wouldn't listen. All of them blindly believed the rumors. Yet something puzzled Madé. For him, it didn't make sense. He always wanted to find out for himself how things worked.

"I'm ready to bet ten rupiahs!" he boldly announced one morning before class. In those days, this was a big sum of money for any child. For Madé, it was all of his savings.

After a lively debate, the challenge was accepted and all the friends agreed that the time had come to investigate. Like detectives, the young princes prepared their plan in secrecy.

After school one sunny afternoon, the boys all marched off in high spirits along the tree-lined road to the center of town where Dutch ladies and gentlemen gathered every day to play their peculiar game inside a very large cage of chicken wire.

When the group arrived, each boy stood there, staring in awe at the strange sight of two men and two women racing madly after a small white ball. Wooden racquets, swinging like clubs, flashed right and left as the players ran up and down the grass. Whenever they stopped, they shouted out a number and then began running all over again.

After debating logistics, the boys found the ideal spot to start their observations. One by one they quietly laid down on the

grass, flat on their backs. Then they carefully pressed their foreheads up against the wire fence. From that vantage point, their eyes could easily scrutinize the female player's legs under their dresses. As they all looked on, a sudden gust of wind billowed up one of the skirts like a balloon, exposing its wearer's bright pink legs. Uncontrollable giggles exploded into fits of laughter.

"You see!" Madé excitedly cried out. "No basket! I knew it!" At that moment, a huge sweating man burst out from the cage, rushing for them, shouting and cursing, furiously waving his racquet like a weapon. All the boys quickly leapt up in a flash and ran for their lives.

Down the road they fled. Howling and laughing, they scur-
ried frantically as the pink monster screamed right behind. They
ran and ran until the tennis man finally turned back to rejoin his
wide-hipped women playing in the heat. Out of breath and out
of danger, the friends all fell to the ground exhausted and elated.

Unanimously, they admitted that Madé had been right
all along. The great mystery was solved. Gedé shook his little
brother's hand in admiration. From that day on, they all were
certain that enormous Dutch ladies with their unbelievably
plump bottoms had no need for fighting cock baskets. And
proud Madé, the young detective, now had twenty rupiahs.

RINGING CRYSTAL

"**B**aangngng..." the sound exploded in the air, sending Madé's heart pounding. A rainfall of musical notes followed in crescendo and then abruptly turned into harmonious ringing crystals that rose from the metallophones. The melody lingered in the night, gaining momentum and then exploding again, shaking the entire *gamelan* orchestra with electric energy. Each note entered nine-year-old Madé, filling him with wonder.

The foreign hotel guests, seated in their chairs, burst into applause after each piece of music, clapping their hands, a strange noisy action which surprised the Balinese crowd who had never seen this happen before. Was it a sign that they didn't like it? Or was it appreciation? No one knew for sure.

It was 1928 and tourism had only recently touched Bali. The Dutch Royal Shipping Company, known as K.P.M., had just finished placing the roof on the first hotel on the island. Visitors, mostly Dutch, sailed all the way from Java's colonial capital of Batavia, today's Jakarta.

Every Saturday morning the cruiseliner docked at the steamy northern harbor of Buleleng. Passengers streamed down and boarded communal taxis that drove the foreigners up the winding road into the cool, cloud-covered mountains and then down into the lush rice-terraced lands of the south. By late afternoon they would arrive at the Bali Hotel.

Evening cocktails and a dance performance welcomed them. That year, an orchestra from a nearby village was considered one of the finest. Its performers specialized in the latest popular music and a dance craze called *kebyar duduk* or seated dancing. Crown Prince Gedé didn't really like the new frenetic style, preferring the more traditional classical music. But ever-curious Madé could not control his fascination. His classmates buzzed excitedly about the weekly concerts. Madé pleaded daily with Bapa Badung. "Please let me go...." The patient old guardian warned him sternly that he could only attend the performance if his brother Gedé agreed to go as well.

So, as you can imagine, there was much persuading to be done by Madé before his cherished brother finally relented to his wish.

When the big day came, the two boys left home escorted by five guardians. Bapa Badung led the entourage as they set out to the Bali Hotel. Although it was still daylight, a large animated crowd had already gathered along the street outside. Balinese onlookers were not allowed onto the hotel grounds. Squeezing their way forward under a sea of arms and legs, the boys finally found a good place by the front gate, and luckily for the two brothers the hotel's stone wall was only a couple of feet high. Because of their royal status, they could not possibly sit down as everyone else would be higher than them, a serious breach in Balinese-Hindu protocol. So they remained on their feet, pressing their chests against the wall.

As the crowd pushed forward, a band of noisy children suddenly climbed on the wall, blocking the boys' view. Madé was quite upset. But he quickly calmed down when an angry-looking waiter stormed out of the hotel lobby and chased the rude kids away.

Then, the boisterous Balinese crowd fell to a hush. The first tourists, wearing large hats and shorts, walked out onto the lawn like a flock of ducks. So many white people together was still a very strange sight. Madé stared curiously at the enormously big guests as they all sat down in rattan chairs, holding their large glasses with drinks.

Darkness fell. Eight hissing pressure lamps, placed high on bamboo polls, now cast a white glow brighter than daylight over the green lawn. One by one, the smartly dressed musicians in colorful *batik sarongs* carried out their glistening instruments. Each sat down on woven rattan mats laid in a circle, allowing enough space in the middle for the dance.

A powerful "BANGNGNG" split the air. Madé held his breath. Sounds of ringing crystal spilled loudly from the *gamelan*. The music rose and fell until out from the shadows emerged Mario, the famous dancer from Tabanan. He swiftly entered the circle, swirling gracefully from side to side. All eyes followed his every move. His head and hands swayed like a flying bird in the wind, dipping and rising with the bewitching music.

Little Madé did not see much of the dance because most of the time the great Mario performed seated on the ground or hopped about in a squatting position. Madé caught only brief glimpses of the dancer's coy expression as he flirted with the *gamelan* players. His golden fan though was always visible, fluttering like a huge butterfly above the orchestra.

In truth, the young prince was not at all upset about missing Mario's seductive gestures, which he found a bit embarrassing. It was not the dancer who mesmerized him, but rather the intoxicating sounds! After the musicians struck their last thundering notes and the crowd drifted off into the warm night, Madé walked home between his wise guardian and his older brother with music ringing in his ears, which would fill his heart for days.

A CULTURE CHASM

Six years had elapsed since Madé's first journey away from home in Minerva, but now a much longer voyage awaited him. There was no high school in Bali, so the king decided to send his sons to East Java. Traveling to the hill town of Malang, long renowned for its high culture and gentle beauty, could not be done by car alone. The restless waters of the Bali Strait had to be crossed.

Weeks before departure, blessings and leave from the gods had to be sought once again and offerings were brought in procession to the seven temples associated with the royal family. Gifts were also prepared for the temples at Candi Dasa and the coastal Goa Lawah bat cave, which was believed to extend all the way underground to the sacred Mount Agung.

But this time they would have to cross over the high mountains through fog-swept Penelokan and bring gifts also to Batur Temple and its gods who ruled over the ancient caldera that served as the water reservoir of the island. Thanks to the breathtaking Lake Batur, the Balinese enjoyed abundant water flow to grow their delicious rice.

Before departing, the king asked the high priest, Pedanda Gedé Putu, to join them. His presence would ensure psychological and physical well-being during their voyage to Java.

For the two brothers, now in their early teens, long trips by car were no longer a novelty. Yet they were filled with great suspense because they had never seen a K.P.M. passenger steamer of the Dutch Royal Shipping Company. After their long winding trip up the mountains and down the other side, the royal group finally reached the northern harbor of Buleleng. Gazing out at sea from the pier, the boys could not believe their eyes when they saw the gigantic white vessel anchored offshore.

One by one, the travelers boarded a stylish motorboat, the high priest first, then the king, followed by the princes and the attendants in order of importance. The boat raced across the waves at top speed. The king smiled, watching his wide-eyed sons. The faster the shore receded, the mightier the ship grew, until a floating white mountain of steel loomed before them, rising out of the sea to touch the sky.

Madé looked happy and so did the crown prince. The only person visibly nervous was the eminent priest whose peaceful expression had changed to fear.

The motorboat reached the waiting vessel and positioned itself beneath a long stairway ramp where the crew, in immaculate white uniforms, waited for the passengers on a small receiving platform. The venerable Brahmin, on the verge of panic, looked at the great ship with the men standing high above him.

In truth, his horrified expression had nothing to do with the stairs or a fear of heights, but rather the contrary. He felt that a grave defilement of his priestly status was about to occur because of all those lower-caste shoes standing high above his head. Unable to contain his distress, he stood up in the wobbly launch and announced that it was simply impossible for him to continue any further, and requested to be taken back home at once.

Madé's father reacted quickly. The king knew that once aboard, each different deck level would create further problems. His mind raced through every possible scenario and then, in a flash of inspiration, he said:

"Your Eminence, unforeseen circumstances at odds with caste status befall each of us sooner or later. Fortunately, something can be done. We must be realistic. When we enter another culture, we must put ours on hold. The only thing to do now is to accept for a while the desecration, which is no fault of our own. This will not matter that much, because from now on Your Eminence will not be required to perform any duties. Once we arrive in Malang and my sons are settled in their new school, we will return to Karangasem. A special purification ceremony will be arranged so that Your Eminence may resume immediately all priestly duties."

Pedanda Gedé Putu listened intently, taking in the words like a deep breath of fresh mountain air. He calmed down and then a smile came over his face. From that moment on, during the entire trip, he never again looked unhappy. The crossings went smoothly and were even memorably pleasant.

A TWIST OF DESTINY

Years passed in the cool Javanese hill town of Malang and Madé graduated from high school first in his class. He had grown into a young man full of idealism, ready to face the world. His luminous dark eyes sparked with curiosity and compassion.

When he returned home to Bali, he told his father about the night when his kind landlady in Java laid in bed with sudden excruciating pain, and he desperately ran outside searching for medical help and could find none. It was then, he said, that he made the decision to become a doctor and to journey far from his ancestors' land to pursue his studies abroad.

The king touched his son's head with great affection and pride but was very sad to hear the news that Madé would be leaving soon. The young prince, in turn, could not conceal his emotions and was visibly moved by the king's compassion.

As Madé packed his bags to depart for university across the oceans, an incident during his early childhood stirred in his memory. He saw himself as a small boy retrieving a red soccer ball from a verandah where the king sat in dialogue with a wise old man from India.

He spoke with his father who confirmed the story of Madé's birthmark and recalled his eminent guest's fateful words: "Your son will meet many dangers in life but will never be harmed. He's blessed with a special protection."

Later that very night, Madé peered into a mirror. In the dim candlelight he saw it, right there in the center of his neck, a tiny dark spot. His birthmark. The voice of the enlightened old man echoed in his mind.

In time, these auspicious words would explain so much when logic failed. These words became a refrain, as familiar as the monsoon rains pouring over Mount Agung, as familiar as the never-ending stream gushing from the holy spring at Tirta Gangga and into rice paddies below his father's water-palace. All seemed part of a larger mystery.

The Indian's verdict turned out to be prophetic. Madé's future unfolded across many foreign lands and seas. Countless dangers brushed close to him. But at each crucial moment, some miraculous turn of events would occur when least expected and, against all odds, to change his destiny.

And ever so often, Madé would remain perplexed at how the old man's eyes had even been able to notice his birthmark in the first place. In truth, it was the tiniest dot the prince had ever seen.

"I slept and dreamt that life was joy.
I awoke and saw that life was service. I served
and understood that with service was joy."

—TAGORE

THE SNAKE OF ASCLEPIUS

No other Balinese had ever studied in Europe, and Madé was the first medical student from Bali to attend the University of Amsterdam. While his fellow students printed their visiting cards, proudly highlighting their student status with the title "Med. Stud," he humbly chose not to do so. Instead, he created a personal *ex-libris* for the books in his growing library.

During his last stay in the palace of Karangasem, just before embarking on his long odyssey to Europe to begin his studies, Madé realized that he did not know the meaning of his own family name, "Djelantik." He consulted the elders of the court who passed their time reading from the old books about the kingdom's history. He even asked the resident shadow play puppet master who knew all the myths. But nobody could give him an answer.

Only then did he dare to disturb his father. After a long sigh, the king said that their family name was the union of *jala* or morning dew, a word from the ninth-century Balinese language, and *entik* or seedling, from everyday vocabulary.

"This is to remind us that our family must be 'life-giving'," he said, "like the morning dew with the seedling." Madé listened with great attention, even though he sensed that perhaps the king was making up the story. Still, he never forgot his father's message of humanism.

One morning in Amsterdam, he woke up with the symbol of his *ex-libris* fixed in his mind. He ran downstairs to his desk and instantly sketched the sun rising from a sea of morning dew. In the middle of his drawing he placed the snake of Asclepius, the symbol of the medical profession, holding a seedling like a rare jewel.

The king's description of *jala-entik* had turned into an image which would accompany his son into the future. Like the morning dew with the seedling, Madé would give life to others.

He did not know then that many decades later, in his older age, he would add color to the drawing: bright golden yellow for the sun, indigo blue for the morning dew and, for the seedling, the vivid green of Bali's freshly planted rice.

FROM HELL TO HEAVEN

The long nightmare of war fell across Europe. The occupying Nazis demanded that all students at the University of Amsterdam sign a loyalty oath. Very few did, of course, and those who refused were hunted down. The Balinese prince went into hiding and eventually ended up on a small farm, where he helped by driving the manure cart and chopping wood.

One morning he received an anonymous letter offering him safe shelter and a clandestine job in the hospital of a small town near the German border. He bade farewell to the farmer's family and rode off on his bicycle.

By the spring of 1943, the prince was still in medical training. In those days of war, British bombers regularly filled the sky like hundreds of silver butterflies glistening high in the clouds. One afternoon, as Madé was coming back home from a weekend spent with friends, he heard the familiar deep, thundering sounds overhead and instantly stopped his bicycle on the country road. Turning his eyes upward, he followed the passage of the planes, all in neat formations. These pilots, he knew, were flying eastward to Germany to drop their bombs on the mighty war installations that were bringing death and horror all over Europe.

Later, as he was bicycling through a town of textile factories, another flock of planes crossed the skies, this time flying west back to England. Strange, he thought, their wings are much closer than usual. The noise was earth-shaking. Then he saw something his eyes had never seen! Small sticks began to fall from the bellies of the bombers. Within seconds, roofs around him burst into flames, explosions rocked the air, and buildings crashed to the ground. A towering wall of fire flared on the road in front of him. Melting asphalt blazed like lava. Quickly, he turned his wheels around to escape the scorching heat. But then a second large wall of fire leapt up before him. He was trapped!

People ran screaming in all directions. The deafening sound of aircraft roared once again. Madé jumped from his bicycle, ran across the road, and flung himself into the doorway of a factory. Inside he saw three men huddled together. Then a giant roar sent the whole building collapsing. Madé opened his eyes. All was pitch black. He could not see. "Oh, my God," he thought, "I'm blind!" And he felt his whole future vanish before him.

Cries filled his ears while he stood petrified on the threshold of the collapsed building. A few eternal minutes passed. Then, miraculously, the veil of darkness lifted, and as the dust settled his sight came back. A cataclysmic scene surrounded him. He stood stunned beneath the doorway. The rest of the brick building was gone. Only the arch above him remained. Behind him, where the three men had been, now was a gaping empty hole.

He rubbed his eyes and touched his body. He was alive! And there, right in the middle of the road, he saw his bicycle. Only the handlebars were slightly twisted. He carefully lifted it up, leapt on the seat, and in a flash began pedaling furiously, maneuvering his way through the rubble and burning asphalt. Finally, he reached the local hospital, a place where he knew he could be most useful. Rushing through the corridors packed with casualties, he volunteered to the chief surgeon who assigned him to the operating room. Madé put on surgical clothes and immediately went to work treating the wounded. Except for brief pauses for

coffee and a sandwich, he worked over sixteen hours without sleep, assisting several shifts of surgeons at the operating table.

Later in the day, over the radio, everyone heard that the bombing had been a mistake. Tragically, the British pilots had misread the maps and thought they were still flying over Germany. "Errors cannot be entirely avoided," said the announcer. "War is war."

The following morning, when the young doctor finally mounted his trusty bicycle and continued on his journey home, he did not feel at all tired. The sun was rising over the wide horizon of gentle green fields. As its luminous rays bathed the canals in silver light, Madé felt his heart expand. Now, more than ever, he knew why he had been put on this earth: to serve human beings.

CUPID'S CHERRIES

Four long years had passed since Madé had left Bali, choosing a different path from his elder brother Gedé. He knew that the Japanese Imperial Army had occupied his beloved island. But that was all the news he had heard. The world of his childhood felt more unreal each day. Deep down, in his heart, he doubted whether he would ever survive the war to see his father and Karangasem again. His nights were filled with anguish and his days cloaked in secrecy.

Upon his arrival in the small town of Almelo, he found safe lodgings in the house of a recently widowed merchant, Mr. Vermeulen, who was a very kind man. One morning after breakfast, as Madé opened the door to go to work, his host stopped him.

"Since you're going to the hospital," Mr. Vermeulen said, "can I ask you a favor?"

"Certainly," Madé replied.

"My friend is very sick with scarlet fever, poor thing. She's a nurse in your hospital. Can you please take this to her?" He held out a red glass jar.

"May I know what's in it?" asked Madé.

"Homemade cherry jam," he replied with a smile. "Deliciously made by my late wife. I'm sure it will cheer up our friend," he winked. "Her name is Astri Zwart. Just leave the jar with the head nurse."

At the hospital Madé went straight to the head nurse.

"Sorry, I've got a shortage of staff," she said in great hurry, "you should take this to the patient yourself. The nurses' sick room is on the top floor," pointing towards the end of the corridor.

Madé climbed the four flights of stairs. When he reached the top, he felt out of breath. A "Do Not Disturb" sign hung next to a door with the name Astri Zwart. He knocked and heard a faint voice: "Ja... ja...."

Slowly he opened the door. A lovely face smiled at him. Instantly, he was overcome by a sensation he had never felt before. He could not utter a word. Everything in the room seemed enveloped in an aura of white. The patient's neck was wrapped in white cotton bandages, the sheets were also white as was her nightgown. Even the steam was white, misting towards her face from a kettle on the bedside table.

Madé was embarrassed yet excited, but did not know why. He felt her eyes gazing at him, both amused and inquisitive. He tried to speak but couldn't say anything. Dizzy and terribly shy, he returned her stare. At that moment he saw her face swirl around him in circles of light.

In a daze he thought he heard her voice asking him, "Who are you? And what are doing in my room?" But, in reality, she had said nothing and this made him even more nervous.

Then, he heard himself pronounce the words "cherries" and "Mr. Vermeulen." At a loss as to what to do next, he did not hand her the gift or even introduce himself. Instead, he placed the precious jar of cherry jam on her bedside table, already cluttered with medicines and the fuming kettle. Then, shyly, he asked her a question: "How do you feel, Miss Zwart?"

Before she could answer, he had reached down for her medical chart at the foot of her bed. But, to his shock, the familiar

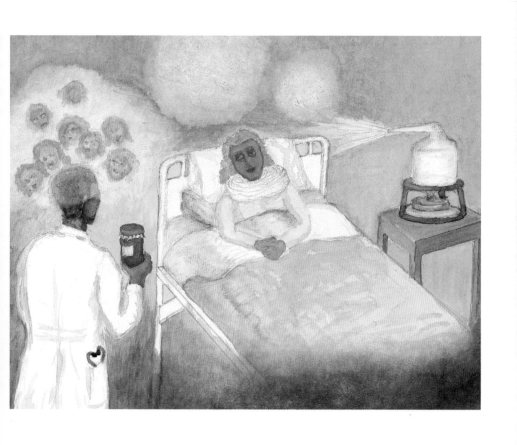

clipboard was not there in its usual place! He did not yet know that hospital rules forbade sick nurses' records to be kept in view.

Embarrassed, Madé was again without words. He simply wanted to vanish. His face blushed red. He realized that the young lady with scarlet fever knew nothing about him. For her, he was only a strange man who had entered her room to pry on her condition. She did not know he was a trainee at the hospital, and he was far too ashamed to tell her.

"I hope you'll get well soon," he finally stammered. He felt foolish and left the room as quickly as possible, running down the stairs with his cheeks on fire and his heart pounding like a drum.

For days the young nurse's face occupied his thoughts. The more he looked back on his awkward behavior, the more embarrassed he felt. He lost his appetite. He fell silent, both at home and at work. His friends did not understand what was wrong with him. They had never seen Madé so withdrawn. Totally new emotions had swept over him, including a strange sense of fear he had never experienced before. Finally, one of his colleagues in the lab heard through the hospital grapevine about the cherry jam he had taken to a nurse.

"Ah, Madé, I know what's wrong with you," his colleague exclaimed in an amused tone. "You must be in love!"

She was right. Prince Madé Djelantik, soon to become Dr. Djelantik, had just made the acquaintance of Astri, the great love of his life, who was destined to become his beloved wife.

A SPLIT SECOND

Not long after his fateful meeting with Astri, Madé had to return to Amsterdam where he continued his studies under cover and eventually passed all the exams for his medical degree. Then he packed his bags once again. In secrecy he traveled across Holland to a town on the eastern border with Germany where he took up a new job, arranged by his underground contacts, in the large hospital of Nijmegen. The ground floor corridor had been turned into an emergency ward, overflowing with wounded men The freshly graduated doctor was immediately assigned to the surgery room.

One evening during heavy German shelling, Madé made his usual night rounds to monitor the newly operated patients. Most nights were relatively quiet, but now he heard the distant rumbling of artillery fire and this troubled him. A voice called out and he stopped at the bed of a young man whose arm was hanging in traction.

"I must lie flat down," the patient moaned, "just for a minute, please!"

In the dim light, the doctor looked at the weight being used to straighten out the man's broken arm and understood why he was in such pain. It was eleven pounds, so incredibly heavy!

Dr. Djelantik was confused. He knew that another doctor's order could not be changed without prior approval. Yet, in spite

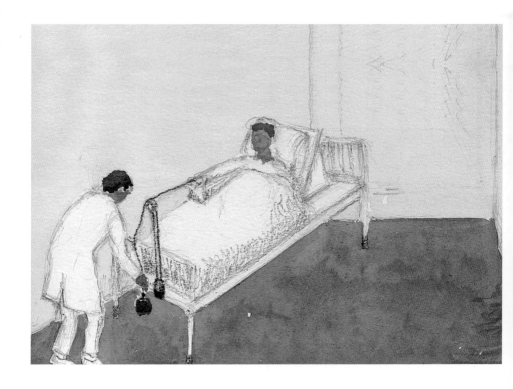

of his commitment to the medical oath, how could he coldly ignore human suffering?

With a few comforting words, Madé tried to assure the patient that his arm would heal only if it remained in traction.

"I'm so sorry," he told him sympathetically, "I can't do what you ask me."

He then turned to continue his rounds. But a moment later, a strange force pulled him back to the young man in pain. How could he possibly help him? Hospital rules were absolutely clear. Releasing the weight would be risky. The broken bones could easily slip out of place. Yet he had to act.

Leaning over, he whispered to the patient, "I'll help you."

"Thank you...," the patient gasped.

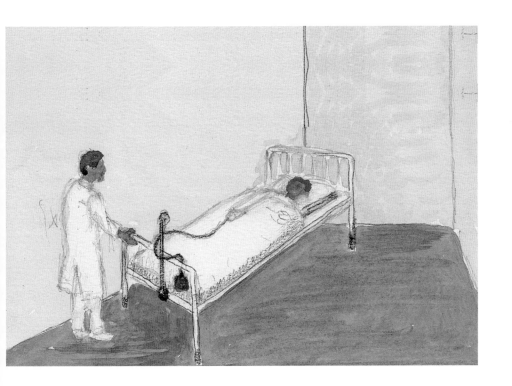

"I'm not allowed to do this," Madé said, "I could lose my job."

The patient smiled through his tears. Madé looked to his left and right. All was quiet. Loosening the rope, he slowly released the iron weight. He removed the wooden support behind the man's back next, holding him upright. Ever so carefully he laid the patient down flat, resting his head gently on the pillow.

"Ooh, doctor, you're so kind...." sighed the young man.

At that very instant, a deafening explosion shook the walls. Wooden fragments, brick, and glass blew across the hall. Madé dove under the bed for cover. Black dust plunged the corridor into darkness.

When the air finally cleared, Madé stood up and brushed all

the debris off the bed and quickly reassembled the traction unit, lifting the patient up, but he found that the man was in shock.

As hospital personnel ran in and out, Madé glanced up at the window opposite the bed. It was gone! Only a big hole remained. Then he noticed a large chunk of smoking metal embedded in the wall right next to the patient. From the metal's trajectory he could tell that the blast had passed directly through the spot where the man had been sitting earlier. Stunned, Madé understood what would have happened if he had not listened to his inner voice.

When the chief surgeon learned about his young doctor's infraction, he called Madé to the office and strongly reprimanded him. He accused him of betraying his oath and turning his back

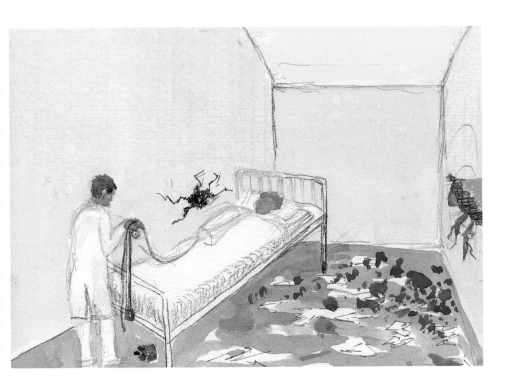

on medical conduct. Madé bowed his head in shame and promised never again to break the rules.

Once he apologized, the chief surgeon then changed his tone of voice and congratulated him for his good fortune in having saved the wounded man's life. This miraculous event gave a huge boost to Madé's morale during those long sad days of war. His birthmark, a wounded soldier, a split second.

HONEYMOON EGGS

The whole of Holland woke from the long nightmare of war with giddy jubilation. Cheers and celebration filled the streets. Madé and Astri's wedding plans added to the excitement of those happy days. Having little money, the couple arranged for a frugal honeymoon on the island of Vlieland off the coast. They planned to camp amidst the most romantic setting they could imagine: a field of wild spring flowers on the shore of the deep blue North Sea.

For three months they saved all their food ration coupons for coffee, sugar, bread, cheese, and ham. Once they had secured their supplies for the weeks of solitary bliss, Astri packed everything in a large box with a good stock of candles, two towels, and their swimsuits. She then went to the post office and mailed the box to the island's harbormaster. Everything was ideally arranged so that the newlyweds would find their precious supplies waiting upon arrival.

Their wedding, on May 31st, was filled with wondrous surprises. Madé's many university friends felt that his marriage deserved extraordinary treatment. Like a theatrical production of a fairy tale wedding, they arranged every detail, from frock coats to top hats, brass trumpets, even a red carpet and, most importantly, a horse-drawn carriage that would carry the happy couple through the streets of Amsterdam! That day, the beautiful Astri took Madé's breath away. As the young Balinese doctor rode in the coach with his bride before a waving and applauding crowd, he truly felt like the luckiest man alive.

After the splendid celebration, the couple set out on their honeymoon and boarded the ferry for Vlieland. After an hour's crossing they docked at the sleepy harbor of their dream island. Once ashore they immediately went over to the harbormaster's office to pick up the box with all their belongings before heading off into the sunset. But the box was nowhere to be found in the sleepy harbor. Everyone searched in vain.

"Well, Madé, at least we have a tent," Astri said, laughing. The newlyweds, without a worry in the world, had little choice but to leave for their camping site without any food.

Armed with only their love and sense of humor, they spent six idyllic weeks in the dunes among wild flowers. Luckily, half a mile away lived a farmer, where they found fresh bread and milk every day. In his daily hunt for food, Madé ingeniously kept always one step ahead of the seagulls and soon learned their habits of laying eggs. For breakfast Astri cooked freshly found seagull eggs, which tasted delicious. Madé would then open up his cherished set of watercolors that he had brought along with an easel. Each day he painted the natural beauty around them.

Only once or twice the couple thought of their missing box, imagining some chubby postal worker back on the mainland feasting on their honeymoon food and sporting Madé's new bathing suit. In the end, the newlyweds became the first nudist bathers on the island of Vlieland.

A MIRACULOUS DOG

Ten years had passed before the prince of Karangasem finally returned home to Bali as a fully fledged medical doctor with beaming Astri by his side. The king welcomed his son with great emotion and pride and kissed his new daughter-in-law. Feasting at the palace lasted many days as Madé shared all his adventures and learned of Bali's great suffering during the Japanese occupation. But the celebration was short-lived.

News came of Made's first posting from the Ministry of Health—Buru, a lost isle in the heart of the Moluccas, hundreds of miles away. The king was horrified and dismayed.

"This is no place for my son," he exclaimed. But for Madé such a remote posting, where no doctor had ever served, was the ultimate challenge. So Dr. and Mrs. Djelantik sailed east into the unknown with their 15-month-old daughter Bulantrisna, "faithful moon."

Approaching Buru's serpentine coastline, the young couple's eyes caught sight of scattered Muslim settlements of Baju sea gypsies and Bugis traders. Inside the deep untamed jungles, they knew, a mysterious people lived far removed from the world. According to legend, these elusive *Alfurus* could become invisible and even fly!

Madé and Astri stepped into their simple wooden house by the bay, feeling like pioneers at the furthest end of the earth.

Their village outpost of Namlea boasted only one vehicle, a Willys Jeep left over from World War II, which belonged to the lonely government administrator who drove up and down the island's only road. Occasionally he could be seen passing by, kicking up great clouds of dust.

Between the house and the road, Madé built a small sandbox under a tree for his daughter and filled it with white sand from the beach. In the soft early morning, before the tropical sun rose too high in the sky, Trisna often played there, allowing her mother time for the daily household chores. Meanwhile, Dr. Djelantik treated his patients in the small thatched roof hut that he had built as the island's first clinic. But all his medical training in tropical diseases had not prepared the young doctor for Buru's many surprises.

One morning, after kissing his wife goodbye, he carried little Trisna out to the sandbox and then headed off to the clinic. But suddenly, as Astri was washing the breakfast dishes, an anguished shriek startled her. She rushed out on the porch, and when her eyes fell on Trisna, her heart froze.

A huge green crocodile had crawled out of the bay and was marching towards her child! As the longest seconds in her life passed before Astri, a small black dog then appeared out of nowhere, running between Trisna and the monster. The massive reptile opened its jaws, baring its sharp white teeth, and the puppy leapt straight into the enormous mouth that slammed shut around it. Thrashing and squirming, the poor trapped creature howled. Ten feet away, baby Trisna quietly watched, her dark eyes open wide.

Astri bolted down the stairs and dashed to her daughter. She swooped her up in one motion and sprinted back to the house. Once safely on the porch with her baby, the shaking mother watched bewildered as the famished crocodile turned around and moved its immense body back towards the beach. Its prey

struggled desperately but was held tightly in its grasp. Aroused by the dog's howls, people rushed to the scene shouting and brandishing machetes, but it was too late. The monster had slipped away, vanishing in the silvery bay.

Dr. Djelantik arrived in a panic. He slowly calmed down his wife and hugged his precious child with great relief. Then he stepped off the porch and walked over to the scene of the crime to study the crocodile's footprints in relation to the sandbox. From where the beast had surfaced on the shore, he could see tracks crossing the road in a straight line, pointed directly at little Trisna's sandbox. He stared down at the terrifying evidence on the sand, and then thought of the little black dog. Where had it come from? He had never seen a dog on the island. And what on earth possessed it to appear at that moment and then leap into the crocodile's mouth? These questions stayed with him because there seemed to be no logical answer for the miracle.

Whispers of *Takdir Allah*—God's providence—soon spread across the island. The people of Namlea did not dare make overt comments about the unseen hand that had saved the doctor's child. But the incredible event quickly enhanced the doctor's reputation.

Not long after, Dr. Djelantik was pleasantly surprised to see many new faces lining up at the clinic for treatment. Even the *Alfurus* had become more open to his ideas about health and disease prevention. All thanks to a miraculous little dog!

NIGHT FUGITIVES

In calm days when the seaborne winds softened, the doctor looked out from his verandah at the tranquil gulf blending into the pale blue sky with no horizon. This view stirred in Dr. Djelantik a peculiar curiosity because he knew it was an illusion. Behind it lay a great mystery. In the far distance, the largest river of Buru Island flowed down the impassable Waingapu jungle valley, emptying its muddy waters into the great bay.

Few people from Namlea had ever ventured to those remote areas. Roads and footpaths did not exist and travel by sea was risky because of sudden storms. Maps were useless. Those shores were infested with hundreds of crocodiles that lay in wait for any passing prey. Yet the doctor wanted to venture there because he knew that no physician had ever gone up the Waingapu River to serve the people. He also knew that many *Alfurus* suffered from elephantiasis, a rare disease he had only seen in medical textbooks.

Finally, his chance arrived. Heavy monsoon rains had lashed the island. Wet winds shrieked in from the sea. And news came from the raja of Waingapu that a doctor was urgently needed. Outbreaks of malaria had stricken entire villages.

Next morning, before dawn, Dr. Djelantik left on his first medical expedition into Buru's wilderness. Twelve porters sent by the raja carried tents, campbeds, mosquito nets, medicines and medical equipment, along with supplies of rice, salt, sweet potato, and dried fish. Two men with sharp machetes led the way, hacking out a path through the jungle. Once inside the great river valley, the travelers waded back and forth through mud and flooding water in a never-ending search for dry land.

Their trek struggled along mile after mile. Dr. Djelantik swatted away large mosquitoes and other insects, while leeches latched onto his tender legs. As night fell, the bedraggled caravan divided into small groups so that each person could find a dry spot to rest on the narrow strips of land still above water.

The doctor felt especially lucky when he came upon what he thought was a perfect spot. The patch of land, ten feet wide, even had a convenient overhanging branch for his mosquito net. The rain had stopped so he didn't even have to pitch a tent. Eagerly, he opened up his canvas bed inside the cozy netting and fell sound asleep.

In the middle of the night, he woke up with a sudden sharp pain on the back of his head. Flashing his torch, he caught a fleeting glance of a small dark shadow. Whatever it was, it disappeared quickly. He searched his bedding, making sure that all was safe before closing his eyes and falling asleep again. But then, just as suddenly, he was jolted awake. His mosquito net shook wildly as if caught in a blowing hurricane. Something was crawling up his leg inside his pants. A rat!

He jumped up, switching on his flashlight. Dozens of rats squirmed around him, madly racing up and down the net. He grabbed a wooden stick off his sleeping cot and frantically lashed out. The rats attacked back, leaping onto his body in a frenzy. Swinging furiously right and left, he hit one of them in mid-air. With an awful shriek, it fell onto his bed in a puddle of blood. Instantly, as if by command, the rats all vanished into the darkness. The startled doctor collected his senses and threw the disgusting rodent out, cleaned up his cot, and lay down in shock.

Next morning, utterly drained from a long night of no sleep, Dr. Djelantik innocently asked, "Did anyone see any rats last night?" Everyone in his party replied "No." They all looked content and well rested. Perplexed, he packed up to continue their trek. Along the way he could not help noticing a curious phenomenon. All the vegetation on some dry patches of land had been flattened, as if a steamroller had run over it. How odd, he thought, and could not understand why.

Many years passed before he found the answer. By chance, a biologist told him how rats migrate en masse during floods.

"They quite simply flatten everything in their way," he said.

Dr. Djelantik realized that he must have accidentally camped right in their path that memorable night in Buru.

"Madé, you're very lucky to be alive today," his friend added. "In times of hunger, migrating rats eat anything that stands in their way!"

RIVER CROSSING

For long steamy days and nights, Dr. Djelantik's medical safari trudged, slogged, and paddled across the wide jungle river valley, seeking out and treating the sick. At the end of each day's march, the group would inevitably arrive at a cluster of abandoned dwellings in the dense forest and pitch their tents. The *Alfurus* always went into hiding whenever strangers approached.

These forest gypsies lived with their own beliefs, unaware of what lay beyond their animistic spirit world. Luckily, one of the porters spoke their language and in time quite a few *Alfurus* timidly poked their heads out of the jungle and into the traveling clinic. Three weeks later, the expedition reached the coast, where isolated far-flung villages could be accessed only by boat. Here the travelers had to reckon with the whims of the sea.

One afternoon, as the men were rowing hard, a blustery wind rose suddenly, preventing Dr. Djelantik's flotilla of four canoes from making any progress at all. The doctor studied his rudimentary map and saw that their destination was not so far away.

After more than two hours at sea, seated uncomfortably on wooden planks in the blazing sun, his body ached all over. All he wanted to do was abandon ship. On his right, a spectacularly white beach with shady palm trees edged out of the thick forest.

Impulsively, he ordered the crew to put him ashore. A village lay a bit further up the flat coastline.

"Go ahead without me," he told his crew. "I'll walk and meet you there."

But his assistant Lamusa insisted, "Doctor must not be alone, I come with you."

So they both stepped out of the boat. When the doctor felt his burning feet touch the cool water and sink into the deliciously soft sand, he was overcome with joy. Stretching his legs, he marveled at the beauty of creation before him. A collection of rose coral and amber shells lay strewn on the blinding white seashore. Behind him rose the dark backdrop of a virgin forest canopy. In awe, he stared at the vision. Lamusa beamed his broad toothy smile. He could hear the voices of the rowers chanting out at sea. He waved back to the canoes that now, a bit lighter, seemed to be picking up speed.

The doctor strolled on with his assistant, stopping now and again when a peculiarly shaped stone or a sea star caught his eye. He found a shiny black coral branch twisted into a small bracelet and he put it in his pocket for Astri. Slowly, he meandered down the paradise beach until Lamusa grabbed his arm, "*Ya'Allah*, by God," he screamed. "Look! Do you see down there? Mangroves!"

Running wildly to the waves, Lamusa whistled out at sea, waving his arms. But the canoes were out of sight. Only then did the doctor realize their problem! Mangrove trees grow only in brackish water. Yes, we must be near a river, he thought. Our boats won't come back for us. We'll have no choice but to cross it.

And sure enough, very soon they faced the broad mouth of a river flowing with the monsoon rains back to the sea. On the opposite side, he could see the village. The doctor estimated the distance—roughly 200 yards. But how deep was the water? He had no idea. He looked at the current. By the soft bluish color, he could only guess that it was shallow.

"Can you swim?" he asked Lamusa.

"No, sir! No!" the scared young man cried out.

"It's not so deep. Perhaps we can walk across," the doctor said, concealing his apprehension. "We can do it, just stay close to me."

The boy's eyes filled with dread as he stripped off his *sarong* and folded it flat. The doctor then tied their two belts together in a lifeline and placed their clothes on their heads before stepping cautiously into the blue-green current. Dr. Djelantik advanced carefully, one step then the other, with Lamusa just behind. But with each new step, he felt the water deepening and the current getting stronger. The boy was terrified as the water grew higher and higher, reaching up to his armpits.

Dr. Djelantik silently began to question himself. What if we have to start swimming? Will I be strong enough to carry him? And what if he starts to panic?

Then, unexpectedly, the river bottom gradually started to rise. With great relief they began walking up a sandbar. Soon the water was up to their waists. Barely had they caught their breath when again they felt themselves sinking deeper into the current.

"Lamusa, we're almost there!" the doctor shouted. The boy did not reply. They struggled on and on and miraculously the water did not rise above their shoulders. The opposite shore was now within reach and they spotted their team setting up camp. Finally, with one last great push, they arrived safely and waded up onto shore.

It was then that Dr. Djelantik noticed a large multitude of people walking towards them. Dripping wet, he hurriedly put on his clothes. Within minutes, the crowd surrounded them. What a sensational reception, he thought, very surprised.

While the *Imam* or village head greeted them with warm respect, the people fell to their knees, chanting. The doctor was amazed. When the prayers came to an end, the *Imam* reached out and gave him a soft handshake. His hand was trembling.

The crowd remained in place staring at both the doctor and his escort, instead of dispersing. The villagers did not move. Dr. Djelantik could not understand why.

Lamusa proudly said, his eyes wide open, "They are thanking *Allah* for our safe crossing. The river is full of crocodiles. *Allah* has saved us. They call you a holy man."

Dr. Djelantik shuddered, remembering baby Trisna's close brush with the crocodile. Then the *Imam*, bowing his head in reverence, uttered, "*Allah* has indeed blessed you!" Dr. Djelantik bowed his head in return.

At dawn, when the doctor awoke from his deep sleep, he heard the soft whispering of voices. Looking out of his tent flap, he rubbed his eyes. There, in the early morning light, stood an incredibly long line of villagers, patiently waiting to receive his medical treatments. And beyond, in the river, his startled gaze fell on a host of crocodiles, their heads rising and falling in the current, staring his way. He touched his birthmark, knowing that he was their prey ... that got away.

MASTS WITHOUT SAILS

A sliver of moon hung low when the dark sea lapped its waves on Buru's southern coast. Dr. Djelantik stood staring at the horizon feeling content because he had cured infections and illnessess in communities that had never seen a doctor.

His expedition was nearing its end and his thoughts turned longingly to Astri and little Trisna waiting in Namlea. He was now more convinced than ever that Astri was the ideal wife for him. Who else would have had the strength to follow him to that god-forsaken island and adapt to such a spartan life? And have the compassion to understand his calling as a doctor?

That night he was a guest of the village chief. Outside his window, under the stars, his men were listening to the villagers' stories. As the night wore on and Dr. Djelantik drifted off to sleep, their laughter slowly gave way to worried whispers.

The next morning his escorts pleaded for a rest. One last sea voyage lay ahead. After fifteen days of paddling, Dr. Djelantik was hardly surprised at their reluctance to continue. However, he thought it was strange that all the young men in the village also refused to accompany him. Finally, the chief persuaded six of them to volunteer with the promise that they would return home the following day. As they left the shore, everyone was serious and silent.

Thankfully, the wind was blowing in the right direction and the oarsmen were pumped with energy. Singing and chanting, they stroked the waves with their paddles in cadence to the rhythm of their songs. The tension melted away as their voices rose to the sky. The doctor loved their songs even though he couldn't understand the words.

The whole scene turned even more idyllic when the speeding canoes rounded a rocky cape lined by a forest of deep shadow and a wide ivory sand beach. The turquoise water was so transparent that the doctor scanned the sea bottom and toyed with the idea of jumping into it. But then, suddenly, an unexpected sight prevented him from jumping into the water for a refreshing swim.

A large sailing vessel with two masts lay resting on the shore, tilting on its side. The masts had no sails. Clearly it was a merchant's boat. Strange, the intrepid doctor thought, where is the crew? He was curious. He ordered the men to pull up on the beach. And then he leaped ashore and marched quickly up to the boat. With the help of his faithful Lamusa, he managed to climb up to look inside. The hull was empty and the boat was stripped bare. But then his eyes saw a body lying under a bench. A dead man! A Chinese, his chest pierced by an arrow! The doctor lost his balance and almost fell. What was he to do? Had the man been murdered? We should dig a grave for the poor victim, he thought. But just as he turned to give orders to his oarsmen, a hysterical scream split the air from one of the men peering over the side of the boat.

"Maati, maati! Dead, dead!"

Howling, he started to run back in the direction of the canoes. His friends followed behind while Dr. Djelantik shouted at them, his face red with anger. This was very unusual behavior for the doctor, who seldom raised his voice

"Stop! Come back!" he yelled. As he stood frozen in place, wondering how he could dig the grave by himself, he heard Lamusa's voice calling him.

"Quick, Doctor! Let's go! They're leaving!"

The men were pushing their canoes into the water and grabbing for their oars. Lamusa was running across the beach screaming, "Stop, Stop!" He then reached one of the boats and was holding it in place with all his might. Meanwhile, the doctor stood on the shore, bubbling with rage. His knees shook as he shouted at the top of his voice, waving his arms, but no one seemed to care. Only Lamusa.

"Dooooc! Please.... Come on!"

At that point Dr. Djelantik realized he had lost control of his men. It was mutiny. And if he didn't act quickly, they would abandon him right there. He had no choice but to run as fast as possible and jump aboard.

In a frenzy the men rowed out in unison over the waves with powerful swift strokes, stirring up the sea. Once far enough from shore, everyone glanced back at the abandoned vessel in the distance. The doctor was still troubled by the crew's behavior.

"Why are they so scared of a dead man?" he asked young Lamusa. "We could have at least buried him? Why did they have to run away?"

The boy looked at his boss in surprise.

"Sir, don't you know why?"

"No," the doctor replied, still disturbed at having left a dead man without burial. It went against all his principles, spiritually as a Balinese-Hindu and ethically as a doctor who had taken the Hippocratic oath.

"It's not the dead man they're afraid of," Lamusa explained. "Last night in the village, everyone was speaking about pirates. That's why so many of your men refused to work today. They heard that pirates are everywhere along these coasts. They hide waiting in the forest. When a boat arrives, they attack without warning, kill the crew and steal everything. Doctor, you saw it. The boat was empty. They even took the sails!"

As Lamusa nervously wiped the sweat off his forehead, he added, "They were probably using the boat as bait."

Dr. Djelantik was speechless. He looked back at the beached vessel and the thick forest. Now he imagined it populated by murderous pirates. If he had been left on the beach, he surely would have met his death! He apologized to his men and thanked them. They smiled back, relieved to be paddling back home, pushing their canoes through the choppy waves. Dr. Djelantik stared up at the billowing clouds overhead and took a deep breath. He realized that once again the hidden hand of his strange destiny had saved him.

ZIEKENVADER'S HORSE

To the delight of Dr. Djelantik, in December 1949 Dutch colonial rule of the East Indies came to an end. However, as the newly founded Republic of Indonesia joined the world community with Sukarno as its first president, revolutionary fervor gripped Asia's newest nation. The entire archipelago plunged into turmoil. Paramilitary groups openly battled with local police and the army across the country. It was at this time that the doctor received word of his new posting in northern Celebes, today's Sulawesi, a huge island in the shape of an orchid floating in the seas north of Bali.

From the very first day the doctor and his wife arrived in Kotamobayu, they were faced with threats and harassment from unruly trigger-happy young men wandering the streets. Yet Astri always managed to lift her husband's morale with her unwavering courage and calm nature. In his quiet, unassuming way, the doctor focused on his primary mission of improving people's health.

Slowly and patiently amidst the chaos, he won over hearts and minds. From the fierce gun-flaunting republicans to the followers of the local raja, from disgruntled colonials to fiery leftists, everyone seemed to appreciate the doctor and his efforts. With no financial help from Jakarta, he designed and built a hospital, which included three polyclinics, two operating rooms, and a maternity ward. Private donations flowed in, especially from the wealthy Chinese community.

Astri did her share of work as well, mobilizing the Ladies Club into civic action. Soon, construction began on the first Maternity and Child Health Clinic in Kotamobagu. The ladies decided to call it "ASTRI," which greatly pleased Dr. Djelantik. By the time the passions of politics had faded and calm was restored, the doctor and his wife's popularity had spread all over the region.

Unlike his days in Buru, he could not abandon his duties at the hospital for long periods of time in the field. But with his expertise in tropical medicine, he was still haunted by the desire to help people in remote malaria-infested areas. Soon, he realized it made more sense to train villagers to become nurses and midwives so they could be posted back home.

The news of his decision spread quickly and eager young men and women volunteers signed up. The doctor greeted the new recruits in their crisp white shirts and began his training program. However, in order to implement his regional "public health" plan, Dr. Djelantik knew he had to visit all of the twenty-eight districts of Mongondow to meet with the village chiefs and select the site for each future clinic.

In those days, venturing upland was an ordeal fraught with danger. Like in Buru, there were no roads. The only way was by foot, horseback, or canoe. For his first expedition, the doctor chose to enter the beautiful Domuga valley, wedged between two steep mountain ranges, where the chief had been expecting him for some time.

The night before his departure something quite strange happened that deeply troubled him. A nightmare woke him up in a cold sweat. In his dream someone was sinking into quicksand. Desperately, the doctor threw out a rope towards the poor man. As the man sank further, his hand caught the rope. It was then that the doctor recognized the face of Ziekenvader, his most trusted assistant! In shock, he woke up and found himself in his own bed covered in sweat.

The terror he had seen in Ziekenvader's eyes stayed with him. He tossed and turned, unable to fall asleep again. Finally, he got up, ate his breakfast, and slowly the dream sank back into his subconscious. Before dawn he was already driving out of town, headed towards the interior.

His team included his loyal elderly male nurse, Ziekenvader, whose name, "father of the sick," suited him perfectly. There was also a midwife, two assistants, and fifteen porters carrying medicines and equipment. By sundown they reached the legendary valley which the doctor had heard so much about. The Domuga chief was there waiting. He welcomed them with coffee and snacks. Generously, he had brought enough horses for everyone as well as a cart pulled by two oxen to transport all the precious medical cargo.

On his horse, the chief proudly led the caravan that followed behind in great spirits, with everyone joking and chatting. Only Dr. Djelantik was silent. He hadn't told anyone that he had never ridden before! Sitting nervously, he gripped hard with his legs, expecting to fall off. But thankfully his horse seemed docile and sure-footed. Slowly the doctor gained confidence and he began to enjoy the vistas around him.

The expedition carefully maneuvered its way through the thick forests and into marshlands dense with high reeds and filled with muddy pools. The doctor's horse plodded along as if it knew the path well, moving safely along the trail. He felt much luckier than Ziekenvader whose headstrong prancing horse would break into a fast gallop whenever the terrain firmed up.

At the rear end of the caravan, the coachman of the cart bellowed and cracked his whip in the air as the oxen plodded along. In this pristine wild beauty, the doctor felt light-headed.

His extraordinary feeling of elation, however, did not last long, because suddenly Ziekenvader's horse bolted away from the main path, stampeding wildly into a marshy pond.

"Stop! No! Come back!" shouted the coachman at the top of his lungs. It was too late. The front legs of the horse had already disappeared in the marsh and the old nurse was thrown off the saddle. The coachman snapped his whip and lurched forward.

"Don't move, doctor, stay where you are," he cried out. Dr. Djelantik sat speechless in his saddle while the horse thrashed desperately, neighing loudly, as it sank deeper in the quicksand as Ziekenvader clung to a floating tree trunk.

The coachman climbed swiftly up a tree with amazing agility. The branches stretched out like an umbrella over the pond. In one toss, like a cowboy with his lasso, he threw a long rope to Ziekenvader who miraculously caught it in mid-air. With the mid-air help of three men, the coachman pulled the nurse back to dry land. Shaken, shocked, and covered in mud, the "father of the sick" embraced his saviors.

"Stay close!" the coachman called out again as the group prepared to move on. Clearly he knew the way along the submerged tracks.

"But what about the horse?" Dr. Djelantik shouted, "Can't we save it?"

"Too deep out there, too dangerous," barked the coachman. "Nothing we can do in that quicksand."

Only the horse's head was now visible, its doomed eyes full of terror. An agonizing howl echoed across the humid marsh. The doctor stared in disbelief as the sinking horse, trapped in the mud, neighed hysterically. Then he looked at Ziekenvader bundled up in a sarong on the cart. A shiver went up his spine. He had seen all this before and vowed not to tell anyone. Then and there, he realized that the terror-stricken eyes of his dream did not belong to Ziekenvader after all but to his horse, which was drowning in his rider's place.

THE CYCLE OF LIFE

U p in the highlands of North Sulawesi, the cool climate reinvigorated Astri. The province of Minahasa had always been a favorite of Dutch settlers. Their coffee, coconut, and cacao plantations extended for miles. But for all the bucolic richness of the landscape, the doctor sometimes wished his eyes could fall on the terraced rice fields of his native Bali.

Although the region was remote, life was surprisingly rich, even cosmopolitan. The Djelantik house soon became a cultural magnet, an inspiring oasis for the educated elite and the European planters who often dropped by to chat and exchange books. Here, the doctor and Astri made many lasting friendships and on their birthdays a profusion of flowers flooded their home, with an endless stream of smiling visitors, arms filled with gifts of cakes and sweets.

An hour by sea from the capital, Menado, a young Dutch friend by the name of Hans Kik lived on the small island of Talisse, managing a coconut plantation. The Djelantiks spent many wonderful days there. By then Trisna had a sister called Surya and they both played with Kik's children, riding ponies across the grassy fields.

At dawn Dr. Djelantik and Astri would wake to the magical sight of fishing boats gliding over gold-flecked waters, their sails flashing in the rising sun. Every morning the fishermen displayed their catch on the stone pier, separating hundreds of tuna fish

into well-tied bundles for the great fish market in Menado.

One day Dr. Djelantik noticed there were fewer tuna and overheard the fishermen complaining. Sharks in the bay, they insisted, were causing trouble. All the fish were fleeing.

Kik's foreman stepped forward, saying that the previous plantation manager, years ago, was famous for his shark hunts. He described his ingenious method of fastening two tin drums at either end of a 50-foot-long cable. In the middle, a shorter cable hung with a huge fishhook dangling off its end. "If you agree, I can make it," the foreman volunteered. Kik gave his immediate approval while the fishermen nodded.

By mid-morning, once all the fishing boats had returned, the foreman appeared with the head of a freshly slaughtered pig hanging from an enormous hook. He jumped into a canoe and rowed beyond the reef. There he lowered the drums, cable, and pig into the water and paddled back as fast as possible.

Dr. Djelantik took out his binoculars and spotted the two floating drums. All was ready.

"Sir, you don't have to stay here, better wait in the house, it may take some time before we hear the sound," the foreman said.

"What sound?" the doctor asked perplexed.

"When the shark swallows the head, he'll swim off, pulling the cables. The drums will bang against each other like mad and you'll soon know when the shark is tired," the foreman smiled. "The noise eventually stops."

"What then?" The doctor asked.

"You wait a little...."

"And...?"

"Well, at that point, if you like adventure, you can paddle out there, pull at the cable, finish off the shark if it's still alive, and haul it to shore."

Dr. Djelantik shuddered at the idea. Yet his friend, his host, beamed eagerly. "What do you think?" Kik asked him. "Shall we go?"

Wanting to please his host, the doctor replied reluctantly. "Well, if you wish...."

"Great!" Kik's eyes glowed with the thrill of the hunt. But the doctor could not bear any form of violence. During his hard years in Buru, he had learned to respect the sea and all its creatures, especially those with big sharp, white teeth. The foreman chuckled, sensing his hesitation.

"You can use those spears," he said, pointing at the lances in the boat. "But be careful. If it's still alive, you must drive the spear in deeply, right behind the gills."

The doctor was concerned. Why did Kik want to go through all this if the foreman was ready to do it, he wondered. And why did they have to harpoon the poor beast?

"I'll hold the rudder and keep the canoe balanced," Dr. Djelantik told Kik, building up his courage.

Then a loud noise echoed from the sea. BANG! BANG! The drums were pounding against each other erratically. People gathered along the beach shore cheering as at the opening notes of a concert.

The foreman warned Kik to be patient. "Don't go out there too early. Sharks are incredibly strong." The banging clanged on for a while. Then all was silent. Two hours passed before the foreman announced that it was safe to go. Kik tapped Dr. Djelantik's back and off they went to the beach. Paddling with pent-up energy, the friends rowed quickly over the glassy water. In only fifteen minutes they reached the spot where the ominous creature floated limp, its white belly exposed to the sun. That monster feared by all fishermen has taken its last breath, the doctor thought. But then, something terrible happened. The enormous body moved.

"My God, he's alive!" Kik cried out, rushing to the prow with a spear. Dr. Djelantik crawled to the stern of the boat. His stomach felt queasy. With an oar, he pushed the canoe alongside the alien mass. When the front of the boat hit it, Kik stood up and drove the spear in with all his might. The thrust jolted the boat, wobbling it from side to side so violently that the doctor almost fell into the water red from the gushing blood.

Strangely, there was no struggle. Kik felt triumphant. The doctor realized that the shark had died before their arrival and that only the waves of the boat had sent the body in motion.

By nature Dr. Djelantik had an aversion to any sport that took away life. But now he thought of the fishermen and all their families that depended on each day's catch. Perhaps this sacrifice was needed after all.

Struggling to pull out his spear from the shark, Kik almost capsized them twice before he attached the stiff metal cable to the

boat. Paddling back with the shark in tow, however, would prove more difficult than flying to the moon.

With each stroke forward, shouting and rowing in unison, the two adventurers did not advance one inch. The canoe was pulled back by the massive weight. After an hour of hard labor, with no visible progress, the doctor's muscles ached while Kik looked defeated, his energy diminishing by the minute. The blazing sun beat down mercilessly. Exhausted, they realized that they had even forgotten to bring water. Dr. Djelantik peered in anguish at the distant shore.

A huge crowd waved at them from the beach. Then he spotted a canoe coming towards them. Help was near! Within minutes the foreman was there with two other men, and fastened a rope to their *prahu*.

Never before had the doctor felt such relief. All his dangerous wilderness treks seemed to pale in comparison to this insane outing at sea. Once they reached shallow waters, dozens of men splashed into the surf to meet them. They dragged the 23-foot-long shark all the way up the beach, cheering with excitement. No one in the crowd took any notice as the two intrepid friends, Dr. Djelantik and Kik, collapsed on the sand.

People encircled the shark. The foreman reached down and sliced open its enormous swollen belly. Suddenly, something incredible happened! A flood of green fluid burst forth, carrying a swarm of baby sharks which darted with slippery swiftness, like quicksilver, in their mad dash to the sea. Children raced after them in wild hysteria, but all escaped. The belly was sliced even further. A soldier's leather boot fell out onto the sand! The crowd cheered yet again.

That evening the entire plantation feasted on delicious grilled shark steak and the fishermen thanked Kik and the doctor for their help. Later that night, as Dr. Djelantik sat with Astri on the verandah looking at the hypnotic movement of silver-lit waves, a fresh breeze off the bay lifted his spirits as he imagined all the escaped baby sharks swimming freely under the moonlight. How many, he wondered, would grow up in this sea to repeat the same eternal cycle of life?

MONGONDOW FOREST

It was midnight when a frantic knock at the front door woke up Dr. Djelantik. Tense, sinister days had fallen on the newly founded Republic of Indonesia. Delirious enthusiasm had turned into burning frustration and anger in the face of broken promises and no assistance. Political parties in Jakarta seemed more concerned with power struggle and political intrigue than the well-being of the nation. Battles raged between armed gangs and the police. Rumors circulated that rival military leaders in the great capital were fueling the conflicts. Rebel uprisings and separatist movements against the weak central government had sprouted across the vast archipelago, and young men had joined in the fighting. In Northern Celebes, it was no different. In those days, when the doctor went to open the door at night, he never knew what to expect.

That evening, on his dimly lit porch, stood two policemen with ashen faces.

"Our patrol has been ambushed along the northern shore. Two of our men are injured and bleeding to death. Please doctor, come with us," they pleaded.

Dr. Djelantik quickly got dressed, opened the garage, and jumped into his jeep. Astri stood at the door half asleep, watching her husband drive off into the ink black night. First, he sped to the hospital to collect medicines and instruments. A nurse joined him as well. The two policemen headed off to get reinforcements. Minutes later, he was driving down dark roads, bouncing over large stones, crossing rivers, and climbing hills in a back-breaking race.

They reached the place of ambush as the light of dawn flickered across the eastern sky. In the grass, four policemen were crouching, with their rifles in combat position. Two bodies lay beside a vehicle. One suffered from bullet wounds and a broken leg. The other was bleeding from a nasty head wound, his leg horribly twisted and broken as well.

The doctor instantly went to work. He pulled out his antiseptics, tools, and bandages. He cleaned the wounds and stopped the bleeding. Then he treated the broken legs with improvised splints. When he finally paused and looked up, he felt an eerie sensation coming out of the dark forest. He was sure that many eyes were watching him, the eyes of armed men hiding behind the wall of vegetation just like those pirates in Buru.

A cold sweat broke out on his forehead as he prepared the injured men for the long trip back. The wounded groaned in pain. For well over fifteen minutes he stood exposed in the line of fire in full view. They're waiting for the right moment to shoot, he thought.

"They won't attack us as long as you're here," one of the patients managed to whisper. Sweat trickled down the doctor's back. The moment seemed to last forever. Finally, he completed the task and packed up his bag.

"We must get them to the hospital at once," he told the policemen, their rifles still pointed towards the menacing forest. One by on they stood up and helped the doctor lift the wounded into the back of his jeep. The nurse climbed in while Dr. Djelantik took his place at the wheel and started the engine. The loud roar broke the heavy torpor of fear. The policemen also jumped in their vehicles and drove off. Bracing himself for a hail of bullets, the doctor

pressed the accelerator. He thought of Astri and the children, and in his heart prayed to the gods of the Bukit Temple back home. Here it comes, he thought! But no shots rang out. He made his way down the winding road. This nerve-racking ride through the Domuga valley forest was the longest twenty-five miles of his life. At every turn he expected an ambush.

At last they reached the hospital and Dr. Djelantik leapt out. The two men were rushed into the surgery room and he began to operate immediately. By the time all was finished, the noon-day sun was filtering through the trees. Drained and tired, he arrived home.

The doctor always stayed above politics. His duties were first and foremost humanitarian. He treated everyone in need in the same way and diligently followed his principles. In time, he got used to traveling with his ambulant clinic across the Domuga valley forest where he would often come across armed rebels. Always suspicious of local authorities, they behaved differently with the doctor and trusted him.

One evening, a leading government official of Mongondow confessed that he was sure that no one would dare to shoot at him as long as Dr. Djelantik was next to him. In his view, the doctor was immune to danger. Hearing these words, the good doctor simply laughed, choosing not to reveal the secret of his birthmark.

FORGOTTEN TREASURE

One day in 1950, the king of Karangasem sent urgently for Gusti Ketut Kobot, a renowned artist from a village near Ubud. Preparations had begun for the *maligya* of the king's late uncle. Without this sacred ritual, his soul would not find its proper place among the ancestors. A painting was needed to decorate the temple and the king wanted to commission an episode from the ancient *Ramayana* epic. Gusti Ketut Kobot was taken aback when he heard the colossal dimensions of the canvas requested—18 x 12 feet—a size far beyond anything the artist had ever faced.

It was both a challenge and a great honor, and Gusti Ketut Kobot accepted. He arrived in Karangasem with four assistants and quickly went to work. For two months they all resided in the palace, painting day and night.

A few weeks later, Dr. Djelantik arrived from northern Sulawesi with Astri and his two little girls, three-year-old Bulantrisna and baby Surya. They had taken their vacation to attend the great ceremony.

Gusti Ketut Kobot's work fascinated the doctor, who observed the artist as he put the finishing touches to the vast canvas stretched out on the floor of the pavilion that had been transformed into an atelier. Under their master's scrutiny, and squatting with their bare feet on the cloth, the assistants were coloring with natural pigments in warm hues the basic figures sketched with charcoal and Chinese ink. The king regularly monitored their work, discussing the deeds of the mythic heroes Rama and Laksamana, who had been so much a part of his sons' childhood fantasies.

Once the artwork was completed, the ceremony took place. And after the ritual had ended, Dr. Djelantik left Bali and had no reason ever again to think about Gusti Ketut Kobot's large painting. The memory of it simply vanished. Years came and went. Twelve to be precise, until 1962 when the doctor returned to the island as chief medical officer of Bali, a position that he accepted with enthusiasm.

One Sunday afternoon as he sat reading on the verandah of his newly built cottage in Tirta Gangga, where he usually spent the weekend, he noticed that heavy monsoon clouds had suddenly gathered in the blue sky. He thought of the brand new Opel Sedan that he had just purchased thanks to a loan from the Ministry of Health. Rushing out to look for something to cover his car in case of a downpour, his eyes fell upon a large bundle of canvas high up on a shelf in one of the garden pavilions. Immediately, he ran to his father, who fortunately happened to be in residence, and asked permission to borrow it. The king agreed and sent his attendants to help lift the fabric down and transport it to the car.

As the men started to unroll it, something unexpected happened. Magical landscapes appeared with lush vegetation, painted figures, and waterfalls. Dr. Djelantik stood in amazement, staring at the extraordinary painting. What was it? Where did this masterpiece come from?

As his mind filled with questions, the sky cleared without shedding a drop of rain. The men rolled up the canvas like a colossal scroll and carried it over to the king's compound, where they unfurled it in front of the old monarch. The king looked on

curiously. Then, as if awakening from a dream, he remembered. A month after the *maligya* ceremony at the palace, the painting had been brought to Tirta Gangga to decorate yet another family ritual. Then it was stored away, never to be seen again.

Dr. Djelantik, too, now recalled having seen the painting before but this time, looking at the myriad of colors, he realized he was faced with a rare work of art. But who had painted it? He simply could not remember. In those days painters did not sign their works. Art was still a communal affair and an artist would never dare to come forward in the first person, as an individual. But suddenly, his father uttered his name, "Gusti Ketut Kobot from Pengosekan."

The doctor was perplexed. Why had such a unique work of art been abandoned on a shelf open to wind, rain, dust, humidity, and to the mercy of red ants? After years of living in Europe, where art was treated with the utmost care, Dr. Djelantik was now faced with an aspect of his own culture which always puzzled foreigners. He, too, like his father, had once taken art for granted. There was an over-abundance of talent on the island. And just as the stone temple carvings deteriorate and decompose, so too was the fate of everything else on the island exposed to the forces of nature.

The tendency of his own people to let precious objects of art fall into neglect, the doctor mused, needed to be viewed, perhaps through the lens of "reincarnation." Every artistic creation has a life of its own—a soul. Any life that dies is reborn. By replacing weathered works of art, new generations of artists are born. How else can creative skill survive and pass from one generation to another?

However, Gusti Ketut Kobot's painting was different. No Balinese artist, he thought, would probably ever have the opportunity to paint such a large canvas again. The doctor's views had changed. He had acquired an almost "humanitarian" attitude

towards works of art. He now believed in preservation and protection and wanted to take care of this painting as if it were one of his patients. Gusti Ketut Kobot's *magnum opus*, he concluded, needed to be brought back to life.

He asked his father for permission to take the painting to his home in Renon, and the king happily agreed. When the doctor left Tirta Gangga that afternoon, his new car was followed by a small pick-up truck carrying the *Ramayana* masterpiece. Once he reached his destination, he unrolled it on his lawn like a carpet and again studied it with tranquil attention. A few days later, he traveled up to the hills of Ubud. The driver parked on the side of the main road, from where the group had to continue by foot. Dr. Djelantik led the way, followed by two young men carrying the painting rolled around a bamboo pole balanced on their shoulders. Descending a steep path, they then proceeded along the narrow dikes separating one paddy field from the other, keeping their balance like tightrope walkers for more than a mile. Finally, they reached Gusti Ketut Kobot's house in the middle of a forest in Pengosekan.

Gusti Ketut Kobot was astonished to see his painting after so many years. When Dr. Djelantik asked him if he could restore it, he scrutinized the canvas and then agreed—on one condition. He needed professional oil paints. Rembrandt tempera. Not an easy request in those days. But the doctor asked Gusti Ketut Kobot to have patience. It would take some time to find the paints. He did not tell him, of course, that he had no idea how to find the Rembrandts.

Patience, Gusti Ketut Kobot would truly need. Two months later, in February 1963, foreboding rumblings of the great volcano turned the eastern sky purple red. In the cataclysmic eruption that followed, thousands perished and even more were injured. The number of displaced reached the staggering figure of three hundred thousand, and it was Dr. Djelantik himself, with Astri at his side, who organized the massive relief efforts.

In the wake of this natural disaster, Gusti Ketut Kobot's painting faded from memory once again. Over two years passed before the island returned to normal. Though many roads and bridges remained destroyed, the Balinese went back to work their rice fields, their lively markets, and their myriad of colorful spiritual activities as if little had occurred to disrupt their lives.

One early morning, Dr. Djelantik was summoned for lunch by President Sukarno, who had come for a few days' rest at his romantic retreat in Tampaksiring. Whenever the beloved leader of Indonesia visited Bali, the birthplace of his mother, he often sent for the doctor whose company he enjoyed.

Sukarno was a true connoisseur of art and an avid collector. That day he asked who, in Dr. Djelantik's view, was the best painter in Bali. Out of the blue the doctor uttered the name "Gusti Ketut Kobot" and in that instant the large damaged painting came to his mind. The president, fascinated by the story of the masterpiece and surprised by its grand size, asked to see the painting. And so barely two hours later, the doctor found himself walking to Gusti Ketut Kobot's house with a retinue of more men than he certainly needed. Not only did he bring back to Bapak Sukarno the forgotten treasure but also Gusti Ketut Kobot himself and his two assistants. In typical Balinese fashion, they all kept humbly at a distance seated on the lawn while their president paced around the canvas, his eyes focused on the *Ramayana* story.

The effect of the painting on Sukarno was astonishing. When Dr. Djelantik told him that, unfortunately, it could not be restored without proper paints, Sukarno reacted immediately. He called the Minister of Foreign Affairs, ordering him to wire at once the ambassador in Rome to send two sets of Rembrandt paints in all colors as soon as possible. When Dr. Djelantik thanked the president, Sukarno replied, "Nonsense! This painting must be saved!"

As the doctor drove home, he reflected on the surprises which life so often has in store. And sure enough, a few weeks later his phone rang.

"Dr. Djelantik, there is a package for you." Recognizing the president's voice, he understood at once what Sukarno meant. The box with the precious oils had arrived. The next day it was delivered into Gusti Ketut Kobot's hands at home in his village.

Yet, the beautiful canvas was forgotten once again because another wave of tragedy swept across the archipelago from west to east, from north to south. Events in Jakarta spiraled out of control. The mythic Sukarno, who passionately loved art and who had helped free the Indonesian people from the Dutch colonial yoke, was overthrown by the army in a coup. Fanning the fire of political hysteria, a witch-hunt of terror began. This time people died, not from natural disasters but from the jealousies and vendettas that divide human beings, and that flared into civil war, all in the name of political power. Tens of thousands were slaughtered each day. Bali's rivers ran red, not from molten lava but from human blood.

No one will ever know how many people lost their lives across the archipelago, but some say over a million. Others claim two, even three. The horrendous purge that began in September 1965 lasted six months. By March the killing fields went silent. The island of the gods once again fell quiet. And life began anew.

One day, when Dr. Djelantik least expected it, Gusti Ketut Kobot showed up at his house with some important news. He had finally restored the painting! Transportation was arranged immediately and the next morning the master proudly reappeared with his great artwork. A memorable day, indeed.

However, nobody in the Djelantik household had ever thought about where to hang the painting, not even Astri. This crucial detail had somehow escaped everyone's mind. No wall in the doctor's house was large enough. After much discussion,

Gusti Ketut Kobot came up with a brilliant solution. Why not cut the painting in half? He would do it in such a precise way that it could be joined together at any time.

The task was accomplished beautifully. The upper part of the *Ramayana* scene, with its volcanoes and hills, was hung in the living room, while the lower part, with rice fields, water springs, and rivers, covered the entire wall of the dining room.

I had admired many times that glorious treasure in Dr. Djelantik's home and often thought about its long adventure. When he would catch me staring at it, invariably he would smile and say, "You see, it serves as a reminder of the enduring power of art and the mysterious workings of *karma*."

A WIND FROM THE EAST

High above the clouds of East Bali rises the mighty Gunung Agung. Every day across the island, all heads turn in prayer towards this most holy volcano, home of the gods under whose protective shadow Dr. Djelantik spent his childhood. After so many years abroad in faraway postings, he gladly returned to his ancestral land to take up the position of chief medical officer of Bali. On clear days, from his house near the bustling capital of Denpasar, he could see the familiar peak of his early years, soaring on the eastern horizon.

For centuries all children had been told that the holy Agung had died long before everyone on the island was born. But, in the month of February 1963, the unthinkable happened. The gods woke up in anger and the volcano came furiously back to life.

All Balinese, young and old, rich and poor, know that when a natural disaster strikes their island—an earthquake, tidal wave, pestilence, or drought—it means that the gods are unhappy with the people, perhaps because of too much greed and corruption. Each calamity is a wake-up call, a divine warning that somewhere the people have gone astray and that negative habits must be cast from their lives.

For three months explosions shattered the peace of the island like rolling thunder. Dark plumes of smoke towered in the sky. Rivers of lava flowed down in a rush to the sea, destroying every trace of life along the way. People fled in panic from their villages on the slopes in search of rice and drinking water, weeping for their lost children and offering prayers to the angry gods. Dr. Djelantik, responsible for all relief efforts and Red Cross operations, worked day and night to save lives, rescue the injured, organize refugee camps, and reunite families. Miraculously, the dreamy water-palace retreat created by his father by the holy spring of Tirta Gangga was spared.

One weekend, during a stay at Tirta Gangga, the doctor and Astri with their children—now four daughters and one son—were kept awake all night by underground tremors and rumblings. The sky above the hills glowed red.

From his father's water-palace, the doctor planned to inspect six Red Cross posts on the volcano's northeastern slope. On Sunday, the weather was gorgeous, the air crisp and breezy. So he decided to take along his ten-year-old boy Widur. Father and son boarded the Land Rover in great spirits, almost as if setting off on a sightseeing tour.

The spectacular drive climbed up winding roads and magnificent green valleys, reminding Dr. Djelantik why his foreign friends always fell in love with Bali. More than once he stopped the vehicle, pulled out his camera and snapped a picture.

But his light-hearted feeling left him as he reached the northern plateau. Dense clouds of black smoke loomed ahead, billowing in immense mushroom clouds, expanding high into the heavens. Stunned, he pulled the jeep over, jumped out with his camera and took a shot of the terrifying explosion. Never before had he seen such an awesome sight. Little Widur stood speechless by his father's side.

Then the doctor's thoughts quickly turned to the Red Cross workers up on the slopes. They must be in danger! He got back into the car and drove frantically in the direction of the columns of smoke.

In the gray dust-covered landscape, he finally reached the first Red Cross station. The volunteers were already taking care of the injured, treating their terrible burns. Blistering lava had suddenly poured out of the crater, catching farmers by surprise in the fields, trapping them in flames. Others, overcome by searing hot air, had fled from their burning houses. Everything within a mile and a half of the flowing lava had gone up in smoke.

Dr. Djelantik checked the patients and planned their evacuation. He then made sure that there were enough supplies of medicines and bandages. As the rumbling died down, he drove back to the coast with his little boy silent by his side. Astri was greatly relieved when she saw her two men arrive safe and sound. All day long she had listened to the distant thunder. Strong tremors had shaken the water out of the pools, flooding the paths all around the water-garden.

A week later Dr. Djelantik went to the only Chinese photography shop in Denpasar to pick up his film. He was amazed to see how well the pictures had turned out. Yet, something really bothered him. One of the most dramatic images was ruined by a white streak that crossed the photo horizontally. What happened, he wondered. Did a flash of light strike the lens? Was his camera defective? Or was it his own error?

A few weeks later, when a team of European volcanologists arrived to study the eruption, they went, of course, to see Dr. Djelantik. He replied to their countless questions and brought out his photos. One of the scientists picked up a picture and instantly asked who had taken it.

"I did," said the doctor, apologizing for the white streak crossing the image. The reaction of the entire group was surprising.

"Doctor," one said, shaking his head, "there's nothing wrong with this picture or with your camera. The white streak is hot gas from the magma!"

"How far were you from the cloud?" another asked.

"I don't know," the doctor replied, shaken, "perhaps a mile."

"Impossible!" one of them exclaimed. "You should be dead."

Dr. Djelantik shuddered hearing those words.

"But doctor," another asked, "didn't you feel any heat from the gas?"

"No, I didn't," he replied, trying to recall the moment. Astri stared at the picture with renewed interest. She then spoke about a similar gas cloud that had poisoned more than a thousand people while they were praying on the southern slope of the volcano.

Later that night, the doctor suddenly remembered an important detail. While he was photographing the cloud, he had felt a sudden gust of wind blowing from behind him with incredible force. Did that powerful wind push back the deadly hot gas? Had Bayu, the god of wind, come to his rescue?

Once again he had been saved.

Against all odds.

CLOUDS OVER BAGHDAD

On the flight back to Iraq after a brief assignment in Karachi, Dr. Djelantik gazed with surprise out of his window. There, on the horizon, floating over the silver green Persian Gulf and the stark Arabian Desert were the most beautiful cloud formations he had seen in years. Spellbound by their magnificent shapes, he reached impulsively for his camera. But then his instinct stopped him.

He had already noticed Iraqi military officers in uniform aboard the plane. Well aware that cameras always raise suspicion in the Middle East, Dr. Djelantik introduced himself to the officer sitting next to him and politely asked if he could photograph the clouds. Colonel Ahmad graciously assented. And the doctor snapped off a few pictures, capturing the spectacular shapes in the sky.

Minutes later, the plane landed in the bustling port of Basra in southern Iraq where Dr. Djelantik had been stationed for over a year working with the World Health Organization in their global fight against malaria. His beloved Astri had not joined him in this United Nations posting. She had stayed behind in Bali to supervise the building of their house near Denpasar. Now, in this faraway land, birthplace of the prophet Abraham, the doctor was alone.

Back in his Basra office, looking out of the window at the

sleepy, flowing Shatt-al Arab River, he took one or two more pictures before placing his camera in the cupboard.

During the next three months, he organized and managed spraying campaigns against malaria mosquitoes across the waterlogged southern marshlands fed by the mythic Tigris and Euphrates rivers. At the end of this grueling period, his colleague Dr. Rishikesh suggested they take a short break.

"A pleasure trip..." the Indian doctor said. "I know a young man whose boat we can charter to navigate the marshes. Winds off the lakes will cool us," Dr. Rishikesh promised, "and we'll see birds of all kinds, wild ducks, even swans."

Before he could finish his description, Dr. Djelantik eagerly replied, "Yes."

That very weekend the two doctors boarded a motorboat for their grand outing armed with tropical hats, sunshades, cameras, lots of water, and sandwiches. The captain, Yusuf, wove his way upriver from Basra, past the oil tankers, freighters, and fishing boats until he turned into a narrow waterway with no vessel in sight.

On both banks thick walls of six-foot-high reeds shielded their passage. Nothing else could be seen for miles and the doctor nostalgically recalled his journey into the Dumoga marshes, years before, when old Zeikenvader lost his horse.

The mysterious watery world of the Marsh Arabs opened before them—a marriage of rivers and reeds in an age-old labyrinth as ancient as Mesopotamia. Advancing through the maze of tributaries, the doctor felt cut off from the modern world. The boat turned in and out, back and forth, until finally Yusuf cut the engine and they glided forward quietly into a large lake. A flock of ducks paddling along the green water took to flight. The pristine nature filled the two friends with delight. As usual, Dr. Djelantik reached for his camera and snapped a few pictures.

But the serene solitude did not last long. All of a sudden, a growling motor's engine broke the spell. Out of nowhere a military vessel appeared and pulled alongside and an officer leapt onto their boat. In one swiping gesture, he grabbed the doctor's camera.

"Pictures forbidden!" shouted the officer.

"What do you mean?" said Yusuf, trying to protect the doctor. "We saw no signs against it...."

Another officer jumped on board as the stern officer was pulling out the film roll from the camera.

"I'm taking it!" he said firmly. "If nothing is wrong, you'll have it back. But first we must see it." Dr. Djelantik nodded, confused, while the man jotted down his name. Then they sped off across the lake and disappeared into a canal. Well, thought the doctor, at least they left me the camera. And for the rest of the day the two friends continued their leisure trip in fairly good humor without giving much thought to the incident.

On Monday morning, a well-rested Dr. Djelantik stepped into his office at the National Institute of Malaria only to find everyone terribly agitated. A colleague nervously announced that two officers of Army Intelligence would soon arrive.

"Two officers from the secret police came looking for you," Dr. Hathat told him nervously. "They have a warrant for your arrest," he added, his voice trembling

The officers showed up five minutes later. Bewildered, the doctor immediately went down the stairs to meet them. But in no time at all he was ushered out of the Institute and pushed into a jeep. They drove to his apartment where he was told to take his toothbrush.

Soon Dr. Djelantik found himself locked in a tiny jail cell with a roof that radiated relentless heat under the scorching sun. Two thin slits served as windows through which no breeze passed. He had no water, no chair, only a beaten cot.

Outside his door he heard a guard shouting in English, "They'll hang you tomorrow!" Totally mystified, he tried desperately to think back to any mistake he may have done. But none came to mind.

After two broiling hours, his colleague Dr. Hathat appeared with food and drink but with no news about the arrest. The army would not answer any of his questions.

"Please," asked Dr. Djelantik, "do something!"

"I'll try," Dr. Hathat promised weakly. But he seemed completely unable to do anything.

That very afternoon soldiers dragged the doctor in for questioning. During the first interrogation, photographs were thrown on the table. He broke out in a cold sweat as he recognized the cloud formations he had taken from the plane months before. And there, beneath his glorious white clouds, in a blow-up photo, he could now clearly see military fortifications along the Kuwaiti border. A shiver went up his spine. They must think I'm a spy! Now, finally, he understood why his life was in danger!

The interrogators shouted with fury, threatening him in their broken English.

"Look at these! Admit it, you spy for Israel! Maybe for Iran! We will break you."

"Let me explain...," the Balinese doctor replied in his quiet voice.

"Don't lie to us!" A huge fist crashed down on the table. The doctor cringed.

"It was an innocent mistake," he insisted.

"Who took these pictures?"

"I did, but...."

"We will hang you!"

Bright spotlights shone straight into his face, blinding him. He heard more voices in the white light but could not see his questioners.

"It was a mistake," he repeated. But all he could hear was the word "spy" and "kill" over and over again. Human moaning sounded from somewhere behind the interrogation room, and soon a long terrible scream of agony echoed through the prison, turning his blood cold.

Keeping his eyes open in spite of the blazing light, he gathered all his courage and spoke.

"It happened on the plane from Karachi," he explained. "A colonel gave me permission to photograph the clouds. This is the truth." As his words flowed out, a great calm overcame him.

The interrogators grilled him again and again. Each time, he took great care not to give a different answer.

"It was an innocent mistake," he kept on saying.

In the middle of the night they came to fetch him again. He was handcuffed and then driven to Basra railway station where he boarded a train bound for Baghdad. Guarded by two army intelligence agents, he sat quietly in a compartment as thoughts of Astri and his children in Bali filled his heavy heart. There was nothing he could do. And no one who could come to his help.

By dawn the next morning, the train pulled into the drowsy capital on the Tigris River. Passing through the iron gates of the dreaded Intelligence Agency, for a last fleeting moment he memorized the sun's dazzling light on the palm trees lining the avenue. As he entered the gray stone portal, he remembered what one of his colleagues had told him. "No person comes out alive from that building." He knew that this might well be his last sight of the open sky.

Once inside, new interrogations began in earnest. During the second questioning, he noticed something strange. The spotlights were not as strong as before. The third round ended with fewer threats of physical abuse. Finally, in the last session, an officer spoke to him in such a friendly manner that Dr. Djelantik was startled.

Then he heard these words that left him speechless.

"I want to apologize on behalf of my government for all the inconvenience...."

The Balinese prince couldn't believe his ears.

"You are free to go."

He looked up into the spotlight as a hand reached out. Standing there, in front of him, was none other than Colonel Ahmad in person, the officer from the Karachi flight. The doctor felt tears swelling in his eyes as they shook hands.

When he walked down the haunting corridors with the colonel at his side, and out into the brilliant sunlight, everything seemed unreal. Passing the armed guards, he nodded ecstatically. Their grim faces kept their scowls.

That morning he took a walk along the Tigris River and thought about the twist of destiny. Without Colonel Ahmad's reappearance, he would have surely ended his life inside a sweltering Iraqi prison, forgotten by the world.

When a soft breeze rippled across the ancient surface of the river, the doctor thought about his auspicious sign. He stopped at a café and stared into a mirror to see whether it was still there at the center of his neck. Yes, there it was! Once again, he knew, the impossible had come to pass.

THE DYING LIONESS

After two years in Iraq, Dr. Djelantik found on his desk in his office in Basra a much anticipated letter from the World Health Organization in Geneva, announcing his new destination. His heart was set on the highlands of Afghanistan, where he had so hoped to be posted. Instead, as he opened the envelope his eyes fell on the word "Somalia." He was urgently needed on the Horn of Africa.

Overlooking the Indian Ocean, the white-washed drowsy port of Mogadishu slumbered far from the world's great events. When the doctor landed, he was the first malaria specialist to arrive there in two years and he began at once to search for a house where Astri could join him. It had not been easy for the couple to live apart as they had done during most of his assignment in Iraq. Finally, in May, Astri arrived with their newly adopted daughter, little Merti Hope. Their other children had already flown away like birds from the nest to further their studies beyond Bali.

The Djelantik home in the United Nations compound was modest but comfortable. Few expatriate families dared to venture away from the coast. Bad roads and very few rest houses kept leisure travel in the vast interior to a minimum.

Somalia's infinite savannah of thorny bush extended for hundreds of miles. Nomadic tribes constantly moved with their cattle in search of grazing lands. Each time they broke camp, they loaded their dismantled *aqal* circular dwellings onto their camels. Water was scarce; rain fell only a few months a year. Often the doctor found himself comparing this thirsty land and its primitive agriculture with Bali's abundant water springs and sophisticated rice culture. These two worlds seemed to represent the opposite extremes of life on the planet.

But to make matters worse, a year after his arrival the rains stopped altogether. Month after month the sun shone brightly in clear skies. Crops burned. Lakes, rivers, and ponds dried up. Cattle collapsed and died. Water became as precious as gold and food was scarce. All across East Africa the earth cracked under the scorching sun rays. The specter of famine loomed over the benighted land. Dr. Djelantik was now faced with a tragedy he could not solve. An entire nation was dying of starvation.

Tens of thousands of refugees sought shelter in the UN built camps of traditional *aqal* dwellings. The roofs of woven grass glistened whitish yellow in the sun. When the doctor entered these homes, he was always struck by the simple symmetrical beauty of the long arching branches, ingeniously crossing each other at the center and planted into the earth to form a perfect circle. But he was also greatly troubled by the suffering of the people who lived inside.

As usual, the biggest problem was water. How to keep the essence of life free from malaria and other diseases in the midst of such misfortune? This was his constant battle.

On one journey he was traveling with his team to a large refugee camp in the northern mountains. The African bush rolled endlessly to the limitless horizon. He had just finished seeding tilapia fish into a number of ponds in the region so that the fish would eat the baby mosquito larvae and stop the spread of malaria. Cattle skeletons littered the rocky terrain. The jeep jolted and bounced along the dirt road.

Suddenly, the driver slowed down. A large lion could be seen in the distance. As they drew nearer, the doctor saw that it was a lioness, completely emaciated, her bony ribs showing through her shriveled coat. She was shuffling along with great difficulty, as if at any moment her legs would buckle. In her agony, she was alone.

Dr. Djelantik could not bear such a miserable sight. He ordered the driver to halt, grabbed his bag of bread and then jumped out of the jeep even before it had come to a halt. But his assistants leapt out after him, shouting.

"Doc, no! You're crazy!" He heard them scream as a host of arms pulled him forcefully back.

"Let me go!" the doctor pleaded, struggling to break loose.

"She's famished and she'll eat you first! Then the bread!" yelled one of the assistants.

The men pulled him back into the jeep as the driver spun the wheel and sped off.

Turning his head around, he looked back at the scene where he had risked his life. "Perhaps they're right," Dr. Djelantik thought. "I must be a bit crazy!"

The exhausted animal was still shuffling forward. Numb from hunger, the lioness hadn't even reacted to the passing engine or the loud shouts of his men. At that moment he realized that not even the prospect of a tasty meal could have reawakened her natural instinct.

This time, the good doctor knew that his protective invisible guardian had exaggerated a bit. For once the roles were reversed. It was the starving lion queen, not the Balinese prince, who was in mortal danger.

BUDDHAS OF BAMIYAN

In the fresh alpine air of Kabul and its changing seasons, Dr. Djelantik and Astri went through their second honeymoon surrounded by the snow-capped peaks of Afghanistan and the river valleys lined with tall poplar trees. The flat deserts of East Africa quickly receded in memory. Gladly, Dr. Djelantik had signed another contract with the World Health Organization and finally his wish had been granted. And now, finding himself in the exact historical crossroads between the Roman Empire, China, and India, his heart smiled blissfully.

In this exotic land he discovered a proud, gracious people, always ready to welcome him with a cup of tea. Whether rich or poor, in elegant villas or in modest mud huts, the Afghanis possessed a true generosity of spirit. They were unafraid of strangers and genuinely friendly. Very often the doctor and Astri took walks through the city's Persian gardens, where families peacefully sat on their wonderfully colored carpets, sipping tea or tasting refreshing *sharbat* while playing with their children.

Adventurous outings in his Land Rover often took the doctor far beyond the capital over rugged mountain passes and across wild landscapes. On one such trip, he and Astri entered into the legendary Bamiyan valley of the ancient kingdom of Kushan where they confronted a sight they both would never forget.

Carved into the rose auburn cliffs, two colossal statues of Buddha stood a hundred and fifty feet tall, watching the world silently from their sheltering caves. Dr. Djelantik and his wife felt as if they were dreaming. Once upon a time, two thousand years earlier, in their moment of glory, these Buddhas had been covered in gold leaf and precious stones. Like regal beacons of spiritual light, they welcomed the travelers who voyaged along the time-honored Silk Route. That afternoon, holding hands, Dr. Djelantik and Astri stared with wonder at those staggering sentinels, silently in awe of the mystery towering above them.

The awesome sight jogged the doctor's memory about another miraculous Buddhist wonder, in Java, the glorious Borobudur temple. Created in the shape of an immense *mandala*, it remained one of Southeast Asia's greatest repositories of ever-renewing spiritual power.

On Afghanistan's high plateau, not long after Alexander the Great's march left its Hellenic traces in the art of Gandahar, the revolutionary philosophy of Buddhism arrived from India. Its roots sank deep into the Afghani soil. And here, at this meeting place of East and West, these sacred giant statues carved in stone still stood proudly as timeless witnesses of the country's ancestral faith. The Bamiyan Buddhas. Holy treasures of the world.

Dr. Djelantik and Astri's long stay in Kabul was enriched by such surprises of profound beauty, natural or man-made. But then suddenly everything changed. Peace was shattered overnight by a *coup d'état* that turned gardens, valleys, and mountain plains into battlegrounds. Dr. Djelantik felt that he was witnessing the end of an era. Afghanistan had begun its long voyage into darkness and agony. He and Astri packed their bags with great sadness and a sense of foreboding. Leaving the country in September 1979, they took with them tribal carpets, copper trays, and many fond memories of the people they had come to love.

Three months later, on Christmas Eve, thousands of Soviet soldiers invaded Afghanistan. A nightmare of bloodshed and violence spread everywhere across the land. The Bamiyan Buddhas, symbols of unchanging truth, silently faced chaos and endless human suffering.

Once again, Dr. Djelantik had escaped by the skin of his teeth.

THE GROWING STONE

Since his return from Afghanistan's lofty altitudes and the desert sands of Iraq and Somalia, Dr. Djelantik had looked at the lush green landscape of Bali through the fresh eyes of a child. At times he felt his heart expand in wonder as if the hand of creation had chosen to give a particular blessing to his ancestral island.

After so much time spent abroad, the doctor retired from his work with the United Nations and now happily opened a private practice in a garden bungalow of the house that Astri had built in Renon, halfway between Denpasar and Sanur. Soon his waiting room was crowded with people from all walks of life, rich and poor. In keeping with his philosophy of affordable health care, he charged very little or nothing for his service.

On the weekend he would escape the hustle and bustle of the southern coast and drive with Astri up winding roads to their wooden chalet in the cool mountain mists of Kintamani, which she adored. Sometimes, instead, they would head east to their little cottage overlooking the water-gardens of Tirta Gangga where grand pools and sprinkling fountains, elephant sculptures and mythical birds all seemed to float in a self-contained sacred world beneath the legendary temple. This magical garden, created by his father, was fed daily by a mysterious spring that took its name from the holy water of the

Ganges—Tirta Gangga. Now the gates of this unique site were open to visitors for a small fee.

Bali was in the flux of change. Some days the doctor would rub his eyes, hardly believing what was happening to the south-western coastal region. The first seeds of mass tourism had been sown. An orderly and calm way of life was being turned upside down. Denpasar already swarmed with traffic pollution. In place of the traditional terracotta pots, women in the villages now balanced plastic buckets on their heads as they walked to and from the water springs. Quiet Kuta had become a noisy tour-ist haven, parading T-shirts and surfboards, sprouting bars and discos. Precious rice fields were disappearing.

"It's only a question of time," the doctor thought sadly. "Soon cement will rise to the sky instead of banyan, palm, and mango trees."

Dr. Djelantik felt that his island, like many other beautiful places on earth, was headed towards a future that remained sus-piciously unpredictable. On the Nusa Dua peninsula, immense hotel projects had broken ground and soon would open their doors to thousands of visitors every year. The potential economic boom had already unleashed aggressive competition. Quick money fueled ambitions, greed, jealousies and, of course, new foreign appetites.

Even in quaint, sleepy Karangasem, things had changed. The old king had died. In his absence, the beautiful halls and covered verandahs of the royal palace, once filled with heirlooms and works of art, had gradually lost their sparkle. The royal fami-ly's power and prestige—its legendary *taksu*—had waned and now lived on only in myth and history. The king's numerous descend-ants had no will to defy destiny and the decline of their own Djelantik dynasty in the face of the modern world.

Yet, amidst all this social upheaval, the doctor noticed that the dynamic phenomenon of *karma* remained unchanged. It affected people's lives in the same inexorable way. No one, whether Balinese or expatriate, young or old, rich or poor, was immune to the consequences of his or her actions. Bali, he concluded, was still very much the home of powerful invisible forces.

His medical calling had long taken the doctor away from his father's court and a feudal way of life, beyond his ancestral origins and caste divisions, beyond nationalities and cultural boundaries. He had bridged all these worlds across the great divide and now spoke the universal language of healing. Over the years, however, he had never lost his faith and had always remained loyal to his Hindu heritage and his family temple in Karangasem.

One memorable morning, Dr. Djelantik drove up to the Bukit Temple with two American friends, Stuart Wilbur and John Breitweiser. On the steep road they passed women graciously balancing offerings on their heads, walking up with their husbands and children, all dressed in festive attire. As always, the doctor did not speak much in the car. His thoughts were turned to every tree, bridge, and stream along the way. Everything was familiar. Distant memories welled up in his mind as if no time had passed since his yearly pilgrimages as a child. The only difference now was the asphalt road and, of course, the delight of not having to walk all day to reach the top of the hill.

As usual, the doctor could feel the story of the temple's "romantic origins" come to life, as if the spirits of his ancestors— the three brother kings and their beloved sister, Gusti Ayu—were present inside the vehicle as it wound its way up the blessed hill. When the car stopped beneath the steep flight of stairs leading to the grand temple, Dr. Djelantik was once again overwhelmed by the gentle breeze that enveloped the air. Silenced by the panorama, his guests looked at the majestic view that spanned the seas all the way to the island of Lombok, its volcanic peak clearly visible.

That day, to Dr. Djelantik's great joy, his beloved older brother, Gedé Djelantik, the crown prince of his childhood, was there waiting for him.

The temple was in great commotion for its forthcoming yearly celebration. Priests, all dressed in white, hurried back and forth, busy with last minute preparations. One temple guardian came to greet them, his hands raised to his chest, palms against each other, and speaking in a subdued voice.

"I must inform you that one of our largest stones here is growing," he announced formally. He explained the phenomenon matter of factly as a supernatural event. In his view the stone had been possessed by a sacred force. A deity must have chosen it as a home. So the priests had enclosed it in a wooden fence to contain its growth but the pressure had cracked the wood.

Dr. Djelantik raised his eyes towards the *kepel* tree born from Gusti Ayu's walking stick. The ancient tree dominated the site with its magnificent height and far-reaching branches dense with the same yellow leaves that once upon a time had turned into swarms of butterflies at sea.

The group followed the guardian over to the "growing stone" at the far end of the temple grounds. The stone—actually a small boulder—stood about three feet high. Its shape was irregular, sinuous, and smooth except for patches of lichens in every shade of green. Offerings of flowers and rice lay below and on top of it. Because of its hidden "spirit," the stone had been dressed up for the occasion with two ceremonial sashes in the sacred colors of white and yellow; tying holy cloth around certain stones and tree trunks is a common practice in Bali.

The doctor looked on in silence. John scribbled something in his notebook while Stuart took photographs. Suddenly, John's voice broke the spell.

"Shouldn't we measure it?" he asked. "In a few years, doctor, you can check again and compare its size."

"Why not?" said the ever-curious Dr. Djelantik. "Great idea!"

Since his early childhood the doctor had never been able to accept a fact without first making an attempt to understand it. Now, more than ever, he felt he had to pursue the test. So John dashed off to fetch a measuring tape which the doctor always kept in the car.

The task of measuring the stone was done by the doctor who proceeded to measure its horizontal and vertical circumferences in their widest spot. On that morning of November 6, 1987, the following numbers were recorded: 73.6 inches horizontally; 52.7 inches vertically. They all agreed that measurements should be taken again at an interval of no less than four years.

For many reasons, not four but seven years passed. Finally, on November 12, 1994, Dr. Djelantik once more drove up to the Bukit Temple with his friends John and Stuart. The doctor held his trusty measuring tape in his pocket like an amulet, ready to check the stone again. Excitement was in the air. This time the temple was not in any festive attire. It was silent except for the breeze gently moving the leaves of the *kepel* tree. Not a soul was around except a lonesome custodian.

The stone now measured 75.5 inches horizontally. John checked his notes and announced, "It's 1.9 inches wider than last time!"

But what really took everyone by surprise was the vertical circumference—62 inches. The stone had grown 8.9 inches! How could this be? The three stood there in disbelief, staring at the gray boulder.

Four more years passed. In 1998, in place of John and Stuart, several of Dr. Djelantik's relatives surrounded the stone in reverence as he measured it. The stone had acquired religious meaning. Just then, a young priest approached.

"What are you doing, may I ask?"

"I'm measuring this rock like I've done twice before. I want to see if it has grown since the last time."

"I can tell you it has," the priest remarked. "The sash I tied around it six months ago no longer fits.... And look here, doctor, the stone is pushing against the tree.... Before there was room for three of my fingers but now the space has gone."

Dr. Djelantik scrutinized the spot carefully. Yes, the stone was firmly pressing against the ancient trunk of a frangipani tree. A small crowd of worshippers now circled the scene. Some women knelt on the ground in prayer, lifting their hands above their heads, palms together, in the *sembah* devotional pose.

On that day, October 28, the stone's width had expanded by 2.75 inches and its height had increased by 3.5 inches.

Puzzled by these findings, and unable to simply accept these facts as supernatural, Dr. Djelantik searched for a scientific explanation. One day, a friend from California sent him copies of a few pages of an interesting book called *Windows of Light* by Randall and Vicky Bear. It described how natural chemical and molecular processes may generate changes in rocks. "If clay picks up just enough organic molecules," the doctor read, "a crystalline structure could develop and as it starts to duplicate, the rock grows...."

Did the stone in the Bukit Temple hold a crystalline structure? The question lingered in the doctor's mind, yet he ignored the answer. Should he share this information with the priests? He decided he wouldn't. He came to the conclusion that the answer was only important for him personally. The priests surely would listen out of respect but then continue making offerings to the deity within the stone. And anyway, he thought, there would always be someone who would ask, "How did this special stone come to settle right here in our temple? And why is it that only this stone has a crystalline structure while the others in the temple don't?" Dr. Djelantik knew that he could not answer these questions.

So, dear reader, if ever you visit Bali and drive to the far eastern region, where many years ago a ball of fire descended like a lantern of sapphire on top of Princess Gusti Ayu's cottage, ask directions to the Kebon Bukit Temple. But don't forget to wear the customary ceremonial sash around your waist. Climb the stairs slowly and, as you enter the gate, you will see looming high before you the majestic *kepel* tree with its magic yellow leaves. And just behind it, a few feet away in the inner courtyard, you will find the sacred stone. In total tranquillity it sleeps and grows.

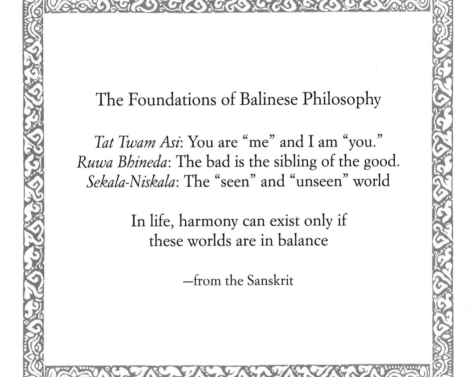

The Foundations of Balinese Philosophy

Tat Twam Asi: You are "me" and I am "you."
Ruwa Bhineda: The bad is the sibling of the good.
Sekala-Niskala: The "seen" and "unseen" world

In life, harmony can exist only if
these worlds are in balance

—from the Sanskrit

The Island That Is No More

One day during a pilgrimage to his ancestral temple, Kobun Bukit, Doctor Djelantik reflected on the drama of life and death. Standing before the legendary *kepel*, he recalled that before the death of his father, a much-loved king, that noble tree had given a warning sign of the coming grieving. All the leaves had fallen, forming a soft carpet all around the base of the trunk. It was the end of an era for the kingdom and the Djelantik royal family, but not the end of the spiritual power residing in the temple.

The doctor smiled at the familiar tree and then walked over to the growing stone. He knew that the sacred stone, too, would preserve its inner spirit and the people's veneration.

Farewell to Astri

Dr. Djelantik could never forget his wife's expression when she attended her first Balinese cremation. Astri, who had converted to Hinduism at the time of their marriage, could not bear the sight of a human body being poked around through the flames to improve combustion. She turned her head away in horror.

"That's when I realized that I had remained Balinese," the doctor confessed to me. "In spite of my long studies abroad and my total immersion in Western culture, I was untouched by the sight. Engraved in my psyche since early childhood was the Hindu notion that the human body is merely the ephemeral outer shell of the eternal soul."

Astri's horror stirred deep compassion in him, but also some anxiety. In January 1967, when Dr. Djelantik's father, the last king of Karangasem was cremated, Astri watched from afar the burning of the bull sarcophagus containing the royal body. In all her years in Bali, she never became used to the way the Balinese treated their dead on the pyres.

"Madé, if I die earlier than you, please do not allow for my cremation to be carried out in such a barbaric way," she pleaded with her husband. And so he complied.

When Astri died in December 1997, she was cremated at the new Taman Mumbul crematorium in Nusa Dua. Surrounded by a large garden, it was the only one on the island. She was the first foreigner of Hindu faith to undergo such a simplified rite of cremation. The spartan ritual was officiated by an enlightened high priest who gave his blessing.

I remember that once the burning was over, the four sisters—Bulantrisna, Surya, Madelief, and Merti—with their only brother, Widur, collected their mother's ashes and took the urn to the sea. The solemn procession made its way onto the beach of Sanur accompanied by the hypnotic sounds of the *beleganjur* gongs and cymbals under an array of traditional white and yellow umbrellas. Then Trisna, Surya, and Widur stepped into a waiting *jukung*, a simple fisherman's canoe with outriggers, and were paddled out to sea. From the distance we saw them casting Astri's ashes into the waves.

Astri's unusual farewell as the wife of a high-caste Balinese raised much debate in the local press and attracted the attention of the entire island. It marked a real break in the habitual traditional Hindu funerary ritual that still represented the greatest financial burden of every family and community.

Farewell to the Melodious Spirit of the Royal Palace

Dr. Djelantik liked often to point out that in this day and age Balinese culture was one of the few that still endowed natural springs, special stones, and trees, even inanimate objects, with a soul! In Bali, all objects of ritual, even masks and musical instruments, contained a "sleeping" power that awoke through prayers and offerings when the objects were in use during festivals.

He told me that the late king's inheritance included a precious set of musical instruments, a small *gamelan* known as *Semar Pegulingang* or "the muse of love." Its exquisite sound was as sweet as the scent of the tiny white *cempaka* flowers favored by the gods. Its fame had traveled well beyond the island. So revered was its tone that his father had commissioned a copy for Queen Wilhemina, and now his precious gift was on permanent display in Amsterdam at the Koninklijk Instituut voor de Tropen, the Royal Tropical Institute.

In his will the king had left the original as a heirloom to all his blood relatives and offspring as if they formed one single "entity," each having equal ownership. The king knew that the hidden power of this *gamelan* was indivisible, elevating it to a higher plane, exempt from the legalities usually tied to matters of inheritance. It could not be divided but only shared.

Throughout his life, his father had treasured this set of percussion instruments and kept it stored away in a high pavilion at the center of the palace. He brought it out only to accompany the gracious movements and subtle pirouettes of the beautiful *legong* dancers in their nuances of romantic love during auspicious ceremonies.

The hypnotic modulations of sound seemed to come from a place not of this world and always lifted the spirits of the entire court, including the musicians, far from earthly concerns. The notes rose to the sky and were heard beyond the palace, touching the emotions of all those who lived nearby, gently cradling the children to sleep.

This *gamelan* was imbued with legend. It was said that the master ironsmith who had forged it well over a century before, had mixed gold with the noble iron, making the notes sound heavenly, a phenomenon that endowed it with inner "power" or *taksu.*

Dr. Djelantik often remembered when, as a child in the palace, he observed the American musician Colin McPhee seated at a table scribbling strange signs on paper while listening to the sweet melody that rose from the "muse of love." Only much later did he discover that this was the language of musical notation, an exclusively Western invention.

After the king's death, the *gamelan* continued to be used only on special occasions. For safekeeping and better protection, it was moved to the personal bedroom of the beloved and much mourned raja.

However, one day in 2002, the year of the Bali bombs, the royal heirloom mysteriously disappeared from its safe shelter. The family was shocked to discover that a young nephew had decided to treat this treasure as his own property. This was a true betrayal of his ancestors all the way back to Gusti Ayu and her semi-divine son, Alit Sakti, founder of the Kebon Bukit Temple. Unbelievably, this irresponsible young man had sold the instruments for cash to settle his gambling debts. In one stunning move, one of the great treasures of the people of Karangasem had been squandered away.

When Dr. Djelantik learnt of the loss, he was heartbroken.

Today, these precious musical instruments lie trapped in the private museum of a brazen Balinese collector who purchased this ancient *gamelan*, knowing full well its royal provenance while ignoring his own *karma*. This magic *gamelan* of intricately carved wood and forged metal is stored inside the walls of a three-story cement building that does not at all reflect the beauty of the artistic objects it contains.

Dr. Djelantik wondered where the *gamelan's* "spirit" that dwelled in its miraculous sound was now. Where was its "soul"? Probably it roamed disoriented in that space of reinforced concrete like a restless, anguished ancestor.

In the end, all Balinese know that every unresolved action will surface sooner or later to demand resolution. It's only a matter of time. And many, in fact, were not surprised when the collector later suffered a stroke and died.

When my mind shifts to the "inner power" of the *Semar Pegulingan*, I travel with my thoughts to many moons ago when

Dr. Djelantik and Astri were staring in awe at the two ancient giant Buddhas carved into the cliff of the Bamiyan valley. They could not have imagined that thirty years later a dynamite explosion by the Wahhabi Taliban, masterminded by Saudi Arabia, would transform those legendary sentinels into monumental clouds of dust. The echo of the blast was heard throughout the world. The immense caves from which those spiritual giants had emerged two thousand years ago are now empty.

Yet, only their visible presence has left us. Their "spirit" is still there, reflected in the cliffs, in every grain of sand, and especially in all the human beings who, from one generation to the next, have lived as neighbors or passed and paused as travelers through that Afghan valley. Perhaps these vanished treasures are even stronger and more present in their absence. They are the void that is forever full. Their ancient spirit lives on within the invisible forces that surround us at all times wherever we may be on this planet.

The Bali Bombs

The 12th of October 2002, the same year the *gamelan* was stolen, is a date which the Balinese will not easily forget. It was their September 11. Bombs set off by Wahhabi terrorists of the group Jemaal Islamiyah killed about two hundred people of twenty-one different nationalities. The explosions occurred at two nightspots in Kuta, a stone's throw from one of the most famous beaches in the world.

Few know, however, that a third bomb detonated minutes later at the American Consulate, ten miles away, just next door to Dr. Djelantik's humble residence. The blast woke up his daughter Surya, shook the glass of the windows, and scared the entire neighborhood. Luckily, it claimed no victims.

Then, the night fell silent again. Mothers put their children back to bed, whispering the old story of how the earth moves whenever the huge restless turtle that carries the island on her back tries to shake it off. But, as the immense weight never falls, she quickly gives up and regains her calmness.

This time, however, everyone understood that the poor turtle had nothing to do with the thundering blast. A new type of misfortune had struck Bali. This was a different calamity, provoked not by natural causes but by human folly.

The doctor was not at home that terrible night. He was sleeping peacefully in his cottage at the holy spring of Tirta Gangga, where he had gone to check on the splendid water-gardens created by his father.

Listening to the radio the next morning, he recognized the voice of the highest religious authority of the island who addressed the entire population. The priest invited each inhabitant to go to the temple to appease the gods. He also suggested that each person turn inwardly and search for the causes of the tragedy.

The Balinese listened and complied. They did not retaliate against the Muslim minority as the bombers had hoped in the intention of spreading chaos and their Wahhabi doctrine across the entire archipelago.

Ten days later, a spokesman for the Kuta communities and nearby villages spoke to a crowd of thousands gathered on the vast white beach.

"What can we do to gain strength from this tragedy?" he asked as hundreds of white prayer flags blew in the wind around the devastation. "Why seek retribution from those who are caught in the web of misunderstanding and anger, who feel that their brutal actions are deeply justified? If we embrace the beliefs, hopes, and dreams of all our brothers and sisters in the world, we can already begin to move out from the *Kali Yuga* 'era of destruction' into the *Kertha Yuga* 'era of justice and peace'.

This is the only weapon we have to defeat terrorism."

As if awakening from a profound sleep, the Balinese began to see mass tourism in a different light. Perhaps this was not the answer to long-term prosperity, nor was Bali independent of the wider world. It was, on the contrary, irrevocably at the mercy of global geopolitics. And whenever tragedy struck, tourists shunned the island.

It was obvious to many that traditional values had been betrayed for the sake of the tourist industry, and much had spun out of control in the name of quick gain. Having evolved at unforeseen speed, the new structures of tourism seemed precariously erected on pillars of ignorance, greed, and illusion. The island's priests, philosophers, doctors, and teachers, all agreed that tourism could only evolve positively if balanced with local faith, tradition, and the environment.

"This is divine punishment because we have not developed a more cultural form of tourism," pointed out Dr. Luh Ketut Suryani, a leading Balinese psychologist. "Instead, we have accepted too many elements that are alien to our culture. Better to serve ten visitors and offer them an exclusive experience than to allow the landing of one hundred vandals interested only in discos, bars, and McDonalds that pollute our island."

In that moment, the population seemed to assume responsibility for the tragedy that had brought their island to its knees. Dr. Djelantik was very proud of their collective Ghandian reaction, most unusual in this age of retribution.

"For Balinese Hindus," he told me, "life consists of striving to reach a balance between the conflicting forces of good and evil."

The real "survivors" of the terror attack, he said, were the farmers who had continued their ancient farming traditions as well as those who had remained connected to their centuries-old culture. The farmers could feed their families and also provide an oasis for those relatives who had left the village but now had lost their jobs in tourism and had to wait out the bad times. Everyone seemed to have understood that the rice fields, the most precious possession on the island, could not feed everyone if sold to developers and turned into cement.

Over the radio, speakers discussed how the earth's natural resources had fallen into the hands of global corporations whose decisions increased the widespread hunger and hopelessness that stood at the root of such terrorism. The Balinese understood that their future was being manipulated by foreign powers. Their solution was a spiritual one.

Now, more than ever, communities poured their energy into their religious celebrations and cleansing ceremonies, paying continuous homage to the gods, hoping to appease them and to return to a peaceful moral renewal.

"The gods of Bali always intervene when the culture falls out of balance," Dr. Djelantik explained to me. "Over centuries, divine forces have always shocked the population back to common sense by awakening the volcanoes, shaking the earth, or sending pests to ruin the crops. Now, even a bomb blast is seen an 'act of God'."

The memory of the deadly events of Kuta entered the collective memory of Bali through a mass cremation ceremony that served as a grand ritual of exorcism. This forced the entire population to reconsider life's sacredness, awakening from the depth of conscience the true foundations of Balinese faith.

"But I wonder if in the future the people will manage to preserve this lucidity?" Dr. Djelantik mused. "And if the governing authorities will finally guide us with wise decisions and rethink this blind subservience to tourism and plan responsibly for the future?"

The Magic Kris

On September 26, 2004, Dr. Djelantik wrote to me:

Dear Idanna,

I have some exciting news to tell you. A group of politicians, business men, intellectuals and artists in Jakarta who support Susilo Bambang Yudoyono—known as SBY—for the coming presidential elections have asked the advice of a paranormal so that SBY may succeed. The medium went into meditation and, after receiving a message from "on high," spoke these words:

"You must elicit the assistance of a powerful ancient *kris* which is in Bali. It dates back to the Majapahit Hindu Empire that ruled Java in the 13th century. The *kris* is owned by a certain doctor named Djelantik who lives at Jalan Hayam Wuruk."

By chance, one in the group happened to be a friend of Trisna. He called her at her home in Bandung, and asked if her father had a *kris* from the Majapahit era. But Trisna knew nothing about it. She then rushed to Denpasar to ask me and was greatly surprised when I showed her the ancient sword of her ancestors. She was even more impressed when I told her the following story:

In 1956, my aged father gathered all his sons in Karangasem to distribute the royal *krises* as part of their inheritance. At that time, I was in Mongondow, Sulawesi and my father completely forgot my existence! Three years later, when I returned to Bali, he called me to apologize for having neglected me.

"I am so sorry, Madé," he said. "I have given all my *krises* to your brothers. However, I still have one left. It's much smaller than the others because it's not Balinese, but probably from Madura." I accepted with gratitude this last heirloom.

Once at home, I started my research. During conversations with my friend, Professor Ernst Utrecht, I learned more about the history of the wars between Bali and East Java. It seems that around the end of the 15th century the Balinese army, under the leadership of my ancestor

Djelantik, conquered the Kingdom of Blambangan, situated across the strait that separates Bali from Java. This was the last Hindu bastion in Java left after the collapse of the powerful Majapahit Kingdom. The victorious Djelantik returned home with a great treasure of jewels, spears and *krises*, and I assumed that my *kris* was part of that.

The leader of that powerful expedition was famed in Bali and known as Djelantik-Mogol. *Mogol* means "unarmed." According to legend, the Balinese had encircled the fortress of the enemy Kingdom of Pasuruan that bordered with Blambangan. Three months passed, but the seige could not bring the enemy to its knees. Then, one night, the leader Djelantik crept unarmed through the main entrance, silenced all the guards, and opened the gates, letting in his army.

Who knows? Perhaps my miraculous birthmark has intervened once again, placing into my hands this magic *kris*. And if now I am telling you this story, it is only because it concerns the current presidential elections. It also shows you how the role of superstition is still so strongly part of the Indonesian mindset.

After my exchange with Trisna, I immediately made arrangements to honor the *kris* with a ceremony in the *merajan* or family temple in the house.

And here is other good news! As you know, despite pre-election polling predictions, the outcome of the presidential election was a landslide victory for SBY, the reformist president. Did the *kris* have something to do with it? Many believe that it did. I am, as usual, skeptical. In any case, I do think that our *kris* is spiritually linked to the events in our nation. For this reason, we have to treat it with great respect.

I've decided to hold the same ceremony in our temple on the day of SBY's inauguration, asking to make SBY strong in his rule of the nation and enable him not to fall in the trap of corruption, and to pursue all the good things for the Indonesian people. I am going to repeat the same ritual on August 17 each year, on Independence Day. What do you think?

Cheers! Madé

Goodnight Sweet Prince

Dr. Madé Djelantik, the royal prince in body and soul, took his last breath at midnight on September 4, 2007, in the hospital of Sanglah that he had founded forty years before. I stood by his side on that night of passage. Surprisingly, the hands of his wristwatch froze in place when his heart stopped beating. And even stranger, the clock hanging on the wall behind his bed also stopped. This I know for certain because I witnessed it with my own eyes.

A week later, on a solemn sunny morning under a pure blue sky, we all gathered—friends, relatives, and a host of Balinese from every walk of life—in the palace of Karangasem in Amlapura. It was the same palace where Madé had played as a child and where the poet Tagore had discovered his birthmark.

Outstretched on a bamboo platform, his body lay draped in white cloth, covered with flowers. Clouds of incense encircled him. Two high priests chanted their hypnotic *mantras* and prayers while shaking intermittently the silver bells as they sprinkled holy water over the doctor in his final rest, his face partly hidden by the white sheet that framed it.

In the afternoon, four male family members, including his son Widur, raised on their shoulders the platform with the doctor's body wrapped in immaculate white and covered with scented flowers. They passed through the lofty entrance just as Madé had done long ago when he descended the stairs to enter the canary yellow automobile, called Minerva, that carried him far away from his childhood home.

The procession advanced solemnly towards the royal cremation ground, led by Widur. As we all filed respectfully in a long line, walking behind the court musicians playing their gongs and cymbals, we moved forward with the crowd as if in a trance under the hot sun. Then something incredible happened. Instead of continuing straight down the hill in the direction of the royal cremation site, Widur bolted to the right into a small ascending road. We all followed, picking up our pace to the beat of the music. The procession wove quickly behind and, as the gong pounded its hypnotic rhythm faster and faster we all found ourselves virtually running behind Dr. Djelantik. After roughly a quarter of a mile, we arrived at a clearing on top of a small promontory and there we stopped, out of breath.

"Where are we?" I asked an old but agile woman next to me.

"This is our cremation ground, for us farmers," she replied. Indeed, it was a simple place.

And then I understood. This had been Dr. Djelantik's last wish.

Our sweet prince did not want the pomp required of his princely status, which all his other relatives craved for. For them the glorious feudal days had not faded. But Dr. Djelantik saw it differently. He knew that the cremation ceremony represented the greatest financial burden on every family. On this day, he wanted to send a message to the Balinese. I could hear his words: "You don't have to spend your life savings to cremate your loved ones. Do it simply. If I can do it, so can you."

And we all stood watching as his body was placed on a small pyre and the wood started burning, quickly turning into crackling flames. His five offspring were present, while all his other relatives were left waiting in vain at the traditional site reserved for the royal caste six miles away in Ujung. Dr. Djelantik had shared his last wish only with his children. He knew that his decision would have breached traditions and created confusion, and that his relatives would not have allowed his cremation to take place in a site reserved for the lowest *sudra* caste. As happened with Astri, this unusual farewell was viewed as a revolutionary act, threatening his royal lineage.

The prince could not have chosen a more humble finale in his Balinese cremation ritual. Now his body was being transformed into ashes on the grounds where the souls of generations of farmers had been liberated by the flames, allowing them to join the eternal cycle of reincarnation.

Once the fire died down, the precious ashes were collected in a bag of white cloth, tied with a yellow gold ribbon. Widur placed it on his head, keeping it balanced with his right hand. He then began to walk towards the seashore, followed by the crowd. The musicians marked the rhythm of our paces for miles until we reached a fishing village at the edge of the Indian Ocean. Powerful waves crashed impetuously against the enormous lava rocks as fearless naked children dove in and out of the restless sea. Their wet skin shone like silver in the sun.

In the distance we could see rows of the colored *jukung* or slender outrigger canoes of the fishermen, waiting on the black volcanic sand beach to be pushed out at sea the next morning. But where we had stopped there was no beach, only boulders and rocks. How could the ashes of Dr. Djelantik possibly reach the depths of the ocean? This question was on everyone's mind. None of us thought about the children.

And then suddenly it all happened. Dozens of kids gathered around Widur, who handed the precious white cloth bundle to a tall boy no more than thirteen years old. We stood there perched like herons on the rocks, all eyes turned towards the scene.

Holding the ashes of our gentle doctor, the boy then braved the elements followed by all the others. We watched their heads appearing in the waves as they swam out like baby sea turtles in an aquatic procession. The precious ashes were raised high above the water as the sun slowly descended towards the horizon.

When the young swimmers had finally reached a certain distance from the shore, the boy's hand rose even higher towards the sky and then he let go of the bundle in the sweeping rotating gesture of launching a fishing net. The ashes of the sweet prince scattered in the wind and then poured down like a flower-shaped firework lit by the golden rays of the setting sun.

And we all said farewell.

So many years have now passed since that hospital night in September 2007 when Dr. Djelantik's watch stopped in unison with his heart. In that strange moment, it seemed as if the world of Bali's mysteries that I had been privileged to witness also drifted away with him. In earlier days, stepping onto the island seemed like entering another dimension. It felt as if creation had favored and blessed that unique corner of the planet. For years I had been held in a stupor of wonder, watching suspenseful tragedies and comedies unfold from season to season under the great volcano in the timeless cycle of *karma*.

Now I look back at this rich ancient culture that once I knew so well and I fail to recognize it. Radical change has mutated Balinese society. So many people now seem disoriented as if they have lost their way in a bad dream, unable to identify even the most familiar road. They grope in confusion as speculation, short-term profit, and pirate behavior have invaded their lives.

Perhaps even Dr. Djelantik would no longer recognize his island that President Nehru called the "dawn of the world." But the doctor, unlike myself, would most likely accept the status quo with quiet wisdom.

On the greater national stage, the hope for a new enlightened president of Indonesia was dashed. The ancient Djelantik *kris* that had contributed its esoteric energy to bring to power the reformist president did not ensure honest and good governance. SBY fell prey to corruption like so many politicians before him.

However, the magic *kris* probably had simply a delayed action because the current president, Joko Widodo, appears to be different from those who have preceded him. He governs with surprising transparency and is loved by the poor for trying to break the endemic corruption that has cursed the country, while forcing businesses and billionaires to pay taxes and minimum wages while respecting workers' rights.

Dr. Djelantik would have been pleased. But the big question is, will this president survive the campaign of generals, oligarchs, and Islamic extremists aligned against him?

The bombs that shook Bali in 2002, forcing the people to face a renewed awareness, did not have the consequences so many had hoped. The doctor was right to view that enlightened moment with skepticism.

In the last decade, a colossal tsunami of greed has crashed upon the island's shores. The extraordinary centuries-old culture that evolved day and night lit by the sun and the moon seems to have closed in on itself like a clam, surviving perhaps only in those few corners of the island where the vegetation still flourishes.

The legendary world of ancestors is being submerged in this modern flood. The island is being stripped of its soul, reduced to another famed escape on the global holiday map with its endless bazaar of cheap trinkets, shoddy bars offering alcohol and drugs, and cement labyrinths encircled by never-ending traffic jams. Dr. Djelantik's unique culture has de-evolved into a pale shadow of itself.

Today, many years after the prince's birth and just over a decade after his death, the *karma* of the island seems to be caught in a vicious circle dominated by the inevitable problems of modernity: abundant garbage, mountains of plastic, and dramatic spikes in cancer and obesity.

In 2010, authorities began lamenting that the island was overbuilt but they did nothing. Privately, instead, they handed out construction permits to whoever could pay New York prices. Every year new hotels rose on precious green rice land so that now six thousand hotels are ready to welcome four million foreign visitors. And this does not include the seven million Indonesian tourists who continually arrive from around the immense archipelago.

Now a sea of advertising billboards lines every road. Storefronts have leapt up like mushrooms. Gray, lifeless concrete has swallowed thousands of hectares of farmland. Precious water is rationed in Denpasar, while golf courses stay green for high-rolling tourists. The entire southern coast has become one urban sprawl.

Today, a surreal mass of shops, cafes, hotels, restaurants, and gas stations crowd the lands from Canggu to Seminyak, from Kuta to Sanur, all the way up into the hills to Ubud.

Where Dr. Djelantik's house once stood, full of charm enshrining the masterpiece by the painter Gusti Kobot, with a garden pavilion framed by an explosion of hibiscus, now looms an immense four-story commercial center complete with escalators and thousands of multicolored neon lights.

Under the immense shadow of the volcano Gunung Agung, under which I have lived for over twenty years on Dr. Djelantik's former land, I watch the rice paddies disappear as my neighbors replace them with albizia trees. When I ask why, they tell me they have no choice. The land can no longer feed their families while the albizia wood is in great demand and the tree grows in only four years without any particular care. Bali's extraordinary culture once based on the sacred rice seed is now threatened with extinction.

I recall when an old friend, the aged Gusti Gedé Raka, a revered dancer and musician from Saba in the district of Sukawati, sat on my verandah gazing at the holy mountain that stood vigilant over the valley and the whole island. He sipped his coffee and then pointed up at Gunung Agung, whose flanks seemed wrapped elegantly in a sash of gentle clouds.

"We live in the time of *Kali Yuga*," he said, "the last of the four epochs, each forming one full cycle through which the universe must pass before it can regenerate itself."

I had heard these words before.

"According to our Hindu faith, this is a time in which civilization degenerates spiritually," the eminent Gusti Raka explained. "But one day, you will see, the gods of Mount Agung will awake the mountain again in furious anger," he warned, looking at the dormant volcano. "The Balinese will then be shaken back to their senses ... but it may be too late. By then all the inner power or *taksu* of their culture will have vanished."

Gusti Raka was deeply saddened by the scandalous illegal sand extraction from the holy mountain that had already begun.

Today, hundreds of trucks continue daily to devour the volcano's lava beds and carry the sand down the mountain to feed the building frenzy on the coast. Meanwhile, each day thousands of visitors land at the vast airport, thirsty for shopping, beaches, discos, and entertainment. Very few know, however, that this globalized "paradise" is still densely inhabited by a pantheon of invisible forces.

Bali has always been the crystallization of invisible forces in constant communication with daily life, in which the "good" and the "bad" are holding hands. Each Balinese, independently from his or her caste of birth, is aware of this and grows up behaving accordingly also in this contemporary time.

Meanwhile, ceremonies unfold everywhere and are more grandiose than ever. Each *Galungan*—the feast in the Balinese calendar of 210 days that marks the gods' descent among the people—the Balinese who work far from home always return to their villages. Globalization might have brought vulgarity and obsessive materialism but it has not succeeded in destroying the strength of the family and the importance of community.

An ancient culture is, by its very nature, complicated. And as in fairy tales beauty is at the mercy of negative forces. The reason for the increased religious fervor in this time of *Kali Yuga* is a continual attempt to keep the gods happy. Everyone knows that the race for money cannot succeed without injuring the environment as well as the original values of society. Everyone knows that the island belongs to the gods and that the Balinese are simply its custodians. And experience has shown that calamities, such as the devastating eruption of the great volcano in 1963 and even the bombs of 2002 are ways the gods choose to punish them and awaken their consciousness. Now more than ever, people fear the anger of their gods and so try in every way to appease them with prayers and magnificent handcrafted offerings and scented incense.

In their hearts all Balinese know that the island has lost its harmony and balance. In the battle between negative and positive forces, the needle of the scale has shifted away from the "good." The Bali of Dr. Djelantik that once was is no more. And while many Balinese have heard through the news that the larger world is also spinning out of control, the people still feel a sense of security from their generosity towards the gods.

Their sacred masks come alive only when worn by dancers performing to entertain the gods during their earthly visit. But behind those masks lies the truth.

This book is my homage not only to the prince but also to the hidden soul of his island.

Delving back in the memory of time, I can say today that I have watched closely the folly of human greed and now suffer in the face of so much defilement. At the same time, I have witnessed so many moments of wonder and enchantment, admired objects of rare artistic beauty, and been so moved by the sensational magic of nature and its vulnerability.

Bali has taught me the art of self-control and the capacity to behave at my best on any occasion while always respecting my own cultural identity. It has also taught me the importance of symbols and ritual, giving me the means to feel at ease in all circumstances and with people from all walks of life and origins.

"Idanna, my friend," the gentle doctor would often tell me, "in life we must strive to become good ancestors. Never forget the words, *Tri Hita Karana*, the cornerstones of Balinese wisdom: living in harmony with God among humans and in nature."

Deep down, Dr. Djelantik knew that the ancient philosophy of life had been betrayed, and perhaps he would not have been surprised when Mount Agung suddenly rumbled to life on August 13, 2017.

As predicted by my late friend Gusti Raka of Saba, the gods unleashed their anger. All the ceremonies of those last years had not placated them. Rolling plumes of ash soared two miles into the purple sky. The airport shut down. Tourists cancelled their vacations. President Jokowi traveled to Bali to show the world that all was under control and open again for business. But the volcano erupted again.

In 1963, when Dr. Djelantik was responsible for saving lives during the last eruption, people refused to leave their villages and, contrary to the official statistics, over thousands suffocated in the deadly ash. Now, entire communities crowded into shelters waiting for the gods' wrath to subside. Many tried to pray at the Mother Temple Besakih. The pull of the invisible world put them at risk from the primordial forces of nature. The cycle of *karma* spun. The island resting atop the turtle's back shook violently. Months later the volcano fell silent. And life continued anew in this changed world.

Personally, I feel that something eternally mysterious will always exist in Bali. But only "those who seek, shall find" as my compatriot Giorgio Vasari wrote five centuries ago about the so-called "hidden Leonardo" behind his own enormous fresco dominating the Hall of the 500 in Florence.

Acknowledgments

This book is also dedicated to my dear friend, the late Joesoef Isak, a a courageous publisher and great man of letters, whose commitment to freedom of the press in Indonesia will always be an inspiration for future generations.

I am deeply grateful to Jennifer Lindsey whose editing touch blessed this new edition; Sarita Newson, my former publisher in Bali for her continuous support; my brother Giannozzo Pucci who published the Italian edition; and the marvelous dancer and doctor, Ayu Bulantrisna Djelantik, who followed in her father's footsteps; her brother, A.A. G. Dharma Widoer Djelantik, and her sisters, Ayu Surya, Ayu Madelief, and Merti Hope.

I also want to thank
Goenawan Mohamad
Francesco Clemente
Stephen Lansing
Kadek Krishna Adidarma
Rasmini Gardiner
Enrica Zaira Merlo
Mary Letterii
Horst Jordt
Cody and Lyn Shwaiko
Rio Helmi
Nyerie Hassal-Abbey
Milo and Ezio Migliavacca
Rodolfo and Yanti Giusti de Marle
I Komang Gedé Astawa

And my late friends from my younger days in Bali
Carole Muller, Wija Wawo Runtu, Hugo Jereissati,
Chris Carlisle, Ruth and Cary Hill, Pierre Poretti,
Madé Wijaya, and Linda Garland.

Published by Tuttle Publishing, an imprint of Periplus Editions (HK) Ltd
www.tuttlepublishing.com

© 2004, 2019 Idanna Pucci

Layout and design: Enrica Zaira Merlo
Original edition: *Against All Odds: The Strange Destiny of a Balinese Prince* (Saritaksu, Bali, Indonesia, 2004)
Photos pp. 10, 13, 17, 21, 26: Courtesy of Mrs. Bulantrisna Djelantik and the Puri Karangasem Historical Society, Bali.
Photo p. 189 by Terence Ward

These stories are based on the true experiences of A.A. Madé Djelantik who has dedicated his life to improving the health of communities in the most primitive and isolated parts of the planet.

ISBN 978-0-8048-5259-3

Distributed by
North America, Latin America & Europe
Tuttle Publishing
364 Innovation Drive
North Clarendon, VT 05759-9436 U.S.A.
Tel: 1 (802) 773-8930
Fax: 1 (802) 773-6993
info@tuttlepublishing.com
www.tuttlepublishing.com

Asia Pacific
Berkeley Books Pte. Ltd.
3 Kallang Sector, #04-01
Singapore 349278
Tel: (65) 67412178
Fax: (65) 67412179
inquiries@periplus.com.sg
www.tuttlepublishing.com

Indonesia
PT Java Books Indonesia
Kawasan Industri Pulogadung
JI. Rawa Gelam IV No. 9
Jakarta 13930
Tel: (62) 21 4682-1088
Fax: (62) 21 461-0206
crm@periplus.co.id
www.periplus.com

21 20 19   10 9 8 7 6 5 4 3 2 1
Printed in China 1907CM

TUTTLE PUBLISHING® is a registered trademark of Tuttle Publishing, a division of Periplus Editions (HK) Ltd.

ABOUT TUTTLE
"Books to Span the East and West"

Our core mission at Tuttle Publishing is to create books which bring people together one page at a time. Tuttle was founded in 1832 in the small New England town of Rutland, Vermont (USA). Our fundamental values remain as strong today as they were then—to publish best-in-class books informing the English-speaking world about the countries and peoples of Asia. The world has become a smaller place today and Asia's economic, cultural and political influence has expanded, yet the need for meaningful dialogue and information about this diverse region has never been greater. Since 1948, Tuttle has been a leader in publishing books on the cultures, arts, cuisines, languages and literatures of Asia. Our authors and photographers have won numerous awards and Tuttle has published thousands of books on subjects ranging from martial arts to paper crafts. We welcome you to explore the wealth of information available on Asia at **www.tuttlepublishing.com.**